FRESH WIND BLOWING

NML NEW MONASTIC LIBRARY
Resources for Radical Discipleship

For over a millennium, if Christians wanted to read theology, practice Christian spirituality, or study the Bible, they went to the monastery to do so. There, people who inhabited the tradition and prayed the prayers of the church also copied manuscripts and offered fresh reflections about living the gospel in a new era. Two thousand years after the birth of the church, a new monastic movement is stirring in North America. In keeping with ancient tradition, new monastics study the classics of Christian reflection and are beginning to offer some reflections for a new era. The New Monastic Library includes reflections from new monastics as well as classic monastic resources unavailable elsewhere.

Series Editor: Jonathan Wilson-Hartgrove

VOL. 4: *"Follow Me": A History of Christian Intentionality*
by Ivan J. Kauffman

VOL. 5: *Longing for Spring: A New Vision for Wesleyan Community*
by Elaine A. Heath and Scott T. Kisker

VOL. 6: *Living Faithfully in a Fragmented World, Second Edition: From* After Virtue *to a New Monasticism*
by Jonathan R. Wilson

VOL. 7: *Plunging into the Kingdom Way: Practicing the Shared Strokes of Community, Hospitality, Justice, and Confession*
by Tim Dickau

VOL. 8: *Against the Tide, Towards the Kingdom*
by Jenny and Justin Duckworth

VOL. 9: *Thomas Merton: Twentieth-Century Wisdom for Twenty-First-Century Living*
by Paul R. Dekar

VOL. 10: *Being Church: Reflections on How to Live as the People of God*
by John F. Alexander

VOL. 11: *A Glimpse of the Kingdom in Academia: Academic Formation as Radical Discipleship*
by Irene Alexander

VOL. 12: *Reforming the Monastery: Protestant Theologies of the Religious Life*
by Greg Peters

FRESH WIND BLOWING
Living in God's New Pentecost

STEVE HARPER

CASCADE Books • Eugene, Oregon

FRESH WIND BLOWING
Living in God's New Pentecost

New Monastic Library 13

Copyright © 2013 Steve Harper. All rights reserved. Except for brief quotations in critical publications or reviews, no part of this book may be reproduced in any manner without prior written permission from the publisher. Write: Permissions, Wipf and Stock Publishers, 199 W. 8th Ave., Suite 3, Eugene, OR 97401.

Cascade Books
An Imprint of Wipf and Stock Publishers
199 W. 8th Ave., Suite 3
Eugene, OR 97401

www.wipfandstock.com

ISBN 13: 978-1-62032-657-2

Cataloging-in-Publication data:

Harper, Steve.

Fresh wind blowing : living in God's new Pentecost / by Steve Harper.

x + 76 p. ; 23 cm. —

New Monastic Library 13

ISBN 13: 978-1-62032-657-2

1. Spiritual life—Christianity. 2. Monastic and religious life. 3. Church. I. Title. II. Series.

BV4501.3 .H37 2013

Manufactured in the U.S.A.

CONTENTS

         Introduction vii
ONE   A New Pentecost 1
TWO   A New Monasticism 21
THREE A New Order 65
FOUR   Exalting Christ 74

INTRODUCTION

If I could send you this book in the form of an invitation, I would do so. That's the way I thought about it as I wrote it, and I hope it's the way you can read and respond to it. An invitation is based on something significant, and the sender hopes that the receiver will say yes and become part of what the invitation offers. As you will discover very soon, I believe God is at work on the earth today in a significant way. There are some places where this is more easily seen, but it is a fact that all of us must take into account. There is a fresh Wind blowing. We are being invited to raise our sails and allow the Spirit to empower and direct us.

Three streams in my life have converged to create this conviction. The first stream is the contemplative tradition. About ten years ago I began to read more directly in that literature, and doing so revived a hunger in me for a simpler and more contemplative way of living. One way that I acted on this desire came in 2009, when I stepped down as the vice president of the Florida-Dunnam campus of Asbury Theological Seminary and became a full-time faculty member. Subsequently, my wife and I have been able to renew the pace of grace in our lives. We have prayed that God's fresh Wind might fill and direct us. We have put our little boat into the water and are trying to be faithful to a more contemplative life that is emerging. We further deepened that commitment at the end of 2012 by retiring completely from the seminary.

The second stream is what some today are calling "a new pentecost." I have joined with a growing number of people in believing that we are living in a significant "kairos time." This conviction has taken me further into a classical Christian spiritual formation that is ecumenical in nature and that gives particular attention to the holy-living tradition. Following this stream is providing me with the joy of increasing my connection to "the great cloud of witnesses" (Heb 12:1) and of establishing my formation in a liturgical way.

The third stream is "the new monasticism." This too is a revival of a classic way of life, but it is being expressed in fresh ways in this generation. To be a monk is to be "singular" (*monos*)—that is, to live for "God alone," but not necessarily in a monastic cell. A growing number of men and women are committing themselves to live as domestic monks—people who live in the world through a variety of vocations, but do so in relation to a rule of life, common vows, mutual accountability, liturgical worship, and compassionate service. I make no claim to be involved in this movement to the extent to which some others are, but the past few years have given my wife and me opportunities to embrace the vision reflected in the new monasticism.

These three streams come together in this book. They have come together before in church history. They can be found in a variety of movements and spiritual orders. I find them underlying my own Wesleyan tradition through the life and work of John and Charles Wesley in early Methodism. I am writing to invite you to join me in a more contemplative way of living—a way of living that moves in response to the Holy Spirit and finds expression in a life of Christian discipleship that incarnates the two great commandments.

I must confess that I feel about myself somewhat the way I felt about Thomas Merton when I first discovered his writings more than forty years ago. He was described as one of the leaders in the civil rights movement. I wondered how he could be so viewed, given that he lived within the walls of a monastery. He was not literally on the cutting edge of the movement, and yet (paradoxically) he was. It was only as I immersed myself in Merton's life and work that I discovered he was a "voice" speaking into the movement from the margin—offering what he once called "conjectures of a guilty bystander."

I see myself that way in writing this book. The bulk of my life has not been lived on the cutting edge of a new pentecost or a new monasticism. And by temperament, I have not embraced what most people mean when they speak of "the contemplative life." I have lived inside the walls of mainline Protestantism and further within what some perceive as the ivory tower of the academy. I have done all this as an ordained member of the clergy, which itself makes up only a tiny percentage of the Christian population.

But as I have done so, I have become increasingly convinced that things must change. And more, I have been blessed to see that they are changing. I have decided to join in. But at this stage of my life, all I can do is hope to be a "voice" God will use to speak this message to some people who have yet to hear it. I write as a "bystander"—even a *guilty* one. But perhaps God can use even that in the larger scheme of things. I pray so.

I have chosen to extend this invitation through a series of meditations, not traditional chapters, so that you can ponder its message, rather than simply read for information. My hope is that this kind of reading will be like a key that opens the door to wider and more personal considerations on your part. If you feel an inclination to join with me in this kind of journey, I invite you to read on.

ONE

A New Pentecost

God doesn't visit the earth occasionally. The Spirit continues to hover over us, perpetuating creation and bringing about new creation. Similarly, Jesus does not visit his Bride—the church—intermittently. We are in constant communion. The church is being continuously renewed. The Spirit is breathing Life into the Body of Christ all the time. This is easier to see when we look back into history than it is when we stop to survey the life of the church in a particular moment. But it is so. The Bridegroom is madly in love with the Bride. We are never separated.

But as with any marriage, there are times of particular and special renewal. There are seasons of refreshing. In human relations we call it "marriage enrichment." In the Christian faith we call it "kairos moments"—occasions when God's time defines and directs our human time. I believe we are living in such a time. I believe we are living in a time when God is doing "a new thing" on the earth. I believe we are living in a new pentecost.[1] I hold this conviction thanks to the insights of others whom I trust, as well as my own observations in the Body of Christ.

But this conviction raises the unavoidable question, what does it look like to be part of a new pentecost? As prayerfully and carefully as I can, I want to offer a response in the form of a contemplative journey in the pages of this book—a journey that will bring us more fully into the ways of God that are unfolding in our lifetime. God is no respecter of persons. No one needs to miss a firsthand participation in what God is doing in

1. When I refer to the biblical Day of Pentecost, I will capitalize the word. When I am writing about the contemporary phenomenon, I will not capitalize the word.

our day. Some of you may be living in actual locations where evidences of a new pentecost are more easily seen. But what I am describing in this book is not limited to living in a particular place; it is an experience with God that can be lived anywhere in the world. I am writing to say to you, no matter where you may be, "Raise your sails and let the fresh winds of the Spirit fill them and take you in directions that will bring new life to you and, through you, to the world."

The Environment of a New Pentecost

To say we are living in a new pentecost requires us first to understand what this means. It requires us to look at the first Pentecost from a different vantage point than is sometimes the case. There may have been as many as a million visitors to Jerusalem for the Day of Pentecost, but there were only 120 believers in the upper room. This means that only one hundredth of one percent (.0001 percent) were directly involved in the outpouring of the Holy Spirit.

This is not where the story of Pentecost typically begins. We call Pentecost the "birthday of the Christian church," but very few people in Jerusalem even knew it had happened. Many people probably walked beneath the windows of the upper room as the tongues of fire fell and the rushing wind blew, totally unaware of what was taking place upstairs. But it was the fulfillment of what Jesus had promised in Acts 1:8 when he said, "You will receive power when the Holy Spirit has come upon you."

Furthermore, when Luke wrote that the believers were all together in one place (Acts 2:1), at least part of the reason for the gathering was that the future of Christianity was by no means certain. There is evidence that at least some of the first disciples were in hiding, out of fear that the same fate which had led to Jesus' crucifixion would lead to their demise (John 20:19). The little band of 120 were clinging to the promise that if they stayed in Jerusalem, something would happen. But they did not know what it would look like or when it would happen.

Again, this is not the way the story of Pentecost is usually told. We have been conditioned to think that the upper room was charged with a kind of "spiritual electricity" and that the believers were "on tiptoe with expectation." But from another angle, they were hanging on by a thread. It turned out to be a steel thread, but at the moment it was happening, they did not know that. Most of the awakenings in Christianity have occurred in these same ways. God does not wait for some perfect time to act. The Spirit always moves in conditions that are a blend of opportunities and obstacles.

The Christians who fled to the desert in the second century did so because they believed the world was collapsing, perhaps even taking the church down with it. About eight hundred years later, monastic reform occurred "just in the nick of time" to keep the whole monastic ideal from dying a painful death. When Martin Luther walked out of the Diet of Worms, he was not thinking, "Now that's a Reformation!" He was trying to figure out where he could hide in order to survive. When John and Charles Wesley were moved to begin the Methodist movement, it was against the backdrop of an Anglicanism that was in the doldrums and resistant to renewal efforts like theirs.

These are the conditions in which a new pentecost occurs. If we fail to see this, we may never realize that a true movement of the Spirit is under way. We will always be looking for something more spectacular, more influential, more prosperous, or more successful. By today's religious standards, the first Pentecost and its successors do not look "good enough." So, we go whoring after a flashier version that will bring out the media in full force and acquire all the celebrity endorsements we think are needed to make it valid.

But this is not a true pentecost. To say we are living in a new pentecost more accurately means we are living in a time when most people will not even notice the new thing taking place—a time when things seem more tentative than guaranteed. We may find ourselves gathering as much out of fear as out of faith. We may have little other to cling to than our conviction that Jesus Christ is Lord. But that is enough. It is what pentecosts are made of. There are peaks in mountain ranges, and there are "peaks" in church history. Yet, as any mountain climber will tell you, the higher the peak, the tougher the climb. In a season of pentecost, there are usually as many reasons to quit as there are to continue.

When I was in high school, the locker room of our football team had a banner over the door through which the team ran out onto the field. The banner read simply, "When the going gets tough, the tough get going." This was the spirit our coaches wanted us to take into every game. This is the spirit God always looks for in order to create another "peak" in the range. The environment of a new pentecost is what it has always been—the way of the Cross.

The Engagement for a New Pentecost

After Jesus ascended into heaven, the apostles traveled the half-mile journey down the Mount of Olives into Jerusalem. All they knew to do was to follow Jesus' instructions to wait in the city until they were given the Holy Spirit (Acts 1:4). As far as we can tell, they did not know what that meant or precisely when it would happen. But they had found Jesus to be honest with them in the past and faithful to his word. They had no reason to stop believing him now.

Likewise, our participation in a new pentecost is not a matter of "wishing and hoping," but rather engaging ourselves in ways that keep us involved in the will of God. It is important for us to see this in the original narrative, because there are always those who believe that we play no determinative role whatsoever in bringing God's will to pass. They downplay the human dimension so that "God can get all the glory." It sounds very spiritual, but it doesn't square with what we find in the biblical story. Luke made it clear that when they returned to the upper room, they carried out significant activities that enabled them to be ready to receive what God had in store for them.

First, they met together. This does not mean that they quit their day jobs and simply "hung out" in the upper room. But it does mean that they didn't separate themselves from each other and become a scattered lot of individual believers in the city. They kept in touch. They did not think of themselves as individuals but as members of a sacred community. When they met together, they most likely listened as various ones of them shared their thoughts and feelings about what was going on. They sought counsel and offered advice. The environment was one of encouragement.

In our day, we are seeing the renewal of community in the Body of Christ. Some of it is occurring in traditional settings (e.g., congregations and monasteries). But much of it is taking place in nontraditional settings such as house churches and new monastic orders. Many of these new expressions are ecumenical in nature as believers emphasize their oneness in Christ more than their denominational or parachurch affiliation.

Pentecostal engagement is about adopting a Kingdom orientation more than an institutional one.

I have experienced the power of this kind of community through a broadening of my knowledge of and participation in Christian traditions other than my customary one. For example, my devotional pattern has become increasingly liturgical and my practices are taken from classic ones found in Roman Catholicism, Orthodoxy, and a variety of Protestant denominations. I am also learning important things from parachurch organizations and from the various expressions of emerging and missional Christianity. Far from feeling that my discipleship is being diluted, I feel that it is being enriched. In addition, I am finding great benefit and inspiration from formative friendships with people who are not part of my particular tradition. Like the first Christians, I believe that we dispose ourselves toward a new pentecost as we "meet together."

Second, they prayed together. Luke says that they were "constantly devoting themselves to prayer" (Acts 1:14). I don't think this means that they never slept, or that they maintained an around-the-clock prayer vigil. I believe it means that prayer was the "atmosphere" within which they worked and waited. They formed a prayer network that kept them attentive to Jesus' promise and preserved their awareness that no matter what was about to happen, God was the source. Just as meeting together was larger than stated times, so also praying together was more than the specific prayer times they shared.

I have developed this view through the teaching of the people I know who live in communities that pray together. Beyond the stated times of prayer, there is also an environment of prayer that saturates their life together. It creates an attentiveness to God and a dependency upon God. When they say that they "pray together," they mean more than the prayer services they attend. They experience the life of prayer, not just acts of praying. And when this occurs, the "veil" between heaven and earth becomes thin.

We need this kind of praying together in order to be a pentecostal people. We have cultivated the ability, especially in North American Christianity, to turn everything into "meetings." Our meetings become boxes, and our boxes become disconnected from one another. When it comes to prayer, we have our "prayer meetings," and we can print in our bulletins exactly when they begin and end. There is no confusion, but there is also no prayer environment that develops over time. We know how to "start" and "stop" almost everything. But when the Bible says that these early Christians prayed together, it means their fellowship was prayerful—whether they were together or separated.

Praying together also means that we seek to step into the stream of a worldwide prayer movement. We take the "our" at the beginning of the Lord's Prayer very seriously, realizing that whenever we pray, we are joining with perhaps millions of other people who are praying at the same time we are. But more than simultaneity, there is a desire to "pray together" about the things that make for renewal and transformation. We want to pray for and with Christians all over the world who are living into the same vision of a new pentecost that we are. The Internet makes this much easier than ever before, as we send and receive messages and as we log on to Web sites that enable us to be part of a global prayer movement. I believe that we dispose ourselves toward a new pentecost as we "pray together."

Third, they tended to business. It's very important that we do not miss this element in the engagement process. We can too easily "spiritualize" our desire for a new pentecost and adopt an attitude that believes the system is so corrupt that the best thing to do is abandon it and go to a remote mountaintop somewhere. There are people today who use pentecostal language but who do so in the context of an anti-institutional sentiment. I do not find this in the narrative leading up to the first Pentecost.

Instead, I find the apostles "taking care of business." And the first order of business was to secure a replacement for Judas. The details do not need to be repeated here, but suffice it to say that Luke provided more specificity as to how they did it than he did to the actual occurrences in the upper room a few days later. If we miss this fact, we miss an essential ingredient relative to engaging ourselves for a new pentecost.

This same spirit can be seen in later pentecostal experiences. For example, when St. Francis of Assisi traveled from place to place, he would not conduct a meeting in a dirty church. He required his followers to sweep the floors, dust the pews, and clean the windows. Only when this was done would he begin the meeting. He believed that God's original instruction to him—"go, rebuild my church"—included the earthly building as well as the heavenly Body. The new pentecost does not understand or support any notion of "churchless Christianity."

Similarly, we engage ourselves toward a new pentecost when we tend to business in institutional Christianity. There is no virtue in abandoning the tangible for the intangible. This only creates a false dualism between the seen and the unseen. If we want to be a people who can live into a new pentecost, we must include in our disposition a willingness to "clean the church" wherever it is dirty.

Whatever we make of these dynamics, the larger point is clear: the early Christians were engaged in activities that enabled them to be ready for the coming of the Spirit. They did not sit idly by, disengaged from the days between the Ascension and the Pentecostal experience. As we seek to be a people ready to participate in a new pentecost, we will not allow passivity to be disguised as spirituality. We will be a people in whom the divine and the human are integrated into a natural expression of faith.

A New Identity

Before I became a professor, I had the privilege of pastoring five congregations. One of my joys in being a local pastor was receiving men and women into membership. Most often it happened after a meaningful process of Confirmation, which only formed a closer bond between me and those who were becoming members. Sometimes the process was highly transformational as people who knew virtually nothing about Christianity came to personal faith in Jesus Christ. On other occasions, it was a "small step" for those who had been nurtured by loving Christian parents and in the fellowship of the church. But however it happened, membership in the Body of Christ was one of the holy moments of ministry.

It's important for you to know the high value I place on membership, for what I am about to say may be unsettling or controversial: membership is not enough. To be a people who live in the new pentecost, something more is needed. A new identity is necessary. We must move from seeing ourselves as members to understanding ourselves as disciples. This does not reduce membership in any way; it only places it in its proper context. The problem with a "membership mentality" is that we can view entrance into the church as the destination. But the truth is that it is only the beginning. Membership is the doorway we walk through in order to begin living the life of a disciple of Jesus.

Imagine for a moment that football stadiums across the country are filled (as they always are) with thousands of fans, all of them eagerly awaiting the game. The teams come out to warm up. The coin is tossed to see who kicks and who receives. The players take their positions. The kickoff is magnificent. The receiver catches the ball . . . and runs into the locker room. A silence falls over the stadium. The crowd waits for an explanation, but none is given. The rest of the players exit the field. Still nothing from the announcer. In a few minutes, fans begin to get up and leave as they realize "that's it." The next morning, they watch ESPN or scan the local newspaper for an explanation, but all they get is a brief story about the great kickoff and where the teams will play their next game.

The following week, stadiums are still largely full. But the same thing happens—a great kickoff, but nothing else. I don't have to go on about this. You know what would happen. Soon, the stadiums would be empty. No one would drive a long distance and pay an exorbitant price to watch a kickoff. Everyone knows the kickoff is only the beginning; there's a whole game to be played after that. Kickoffs are necessary, but they are only the starting point.

In the same way, being "born again" through baptism and profession of faith is only the beginning.[2] New birth doesn't make much sense if there is no ongoing life that follows it. Similarly, people who stop with membership fail to live as God intended for them to live. When the emphasis is put on membership, we immediately begin to think of who is "in," and that means (in some way) everyone else is "out." When the emphasis is put upon membership, we must now turn our attention to defining what it means to be a "good member" of the institution (rather than a child of the Kingdom), and we are required to provide "good programs" for the members like other organizations do.

A membership mentality also puts great pressure on individual congregations to look at others as competitors, rather than co-laborers with Christ. The goal is to "get members," and so we have to market ourselves more effectively than others do and have better facilities and events than others do so that people will be attracted to "us" rather than to "them." All this costs money, so that the economic demands weigh increasingly heavy on pastor and people. Maintenance eclipses mission; preservation becomes the unspoken goal more than penetration into the culture as salt, light, and leaven. I've spent more than forty years in institutional Christianity, and I've talked with a lot of leaders. Many of us are tired, and we are

---

2. I have connected baptism and profession of faith as a reminder that all Christian groups include both dimensions in some way. Infant baptism is followed by Confirmation. Adult-believer baptism puts the water and the witness into the same experience.

beset by the niggling feeling that Jesus did not come into the world to die for or to establish much of what we devote our time and energy to.

The greatest example of what happens when membership eclipses discipleship can be seen in the religious leaders of Jesus' day. The Messiah was right in front of them, but their definitions of "membership" clearly revealed that Jesus didn't fit the picture. And when push came to shove, they chose their membership paradigm over God's revelation. That's what happens when a membership mentality goes to seed. It's why many Christians continue to hold to the mistaken notion that faith and membership are the same thing.

I found this out firsthand in the first church I served after graduating from seminary. One evening in a small group, I asked those present to name the apostles. We got the Twelve in pretty short order. I then repeated my request, asking them once more to name the apostles. A few looked at me as if to say, "I thought we already did that," but they played along, figuring that I wanted them to name people like Paul, Lydia, or Timothy. Other biblical names followed. When silence fell, again I said, "Name the apostles." Now the looks on their faces really communicated confusion. A few more names came forth, and I said one last time, "Name the apostles."

Kiefer, a longtime and devoted member of the church, sat silent in the group, looking at me with something like exasperation. But he knew there was a method to my madness, so he asked, "What do you want, pastor? Do you want us to put *our* names on that list?" I immediately replied, "Yes, that's exactly what I want! I want every one of us to put our name on the list." The good news is that Kiefer got it, and he did it. That was more than thirty-five years ago, but if you met Kiefer today, he would tell you that evening was a turning point in his life. It was the moment he saw the difference between membership and discipleship—and he decided to follow Jesus for the rest of his life as a disciple, not simply as a member.

Do not forget that I began this meditation with a clear and unmistakable affirmation of membership. Every membership liturgy I know asks key questions and asks for vows that express serious commitments. But we are not ultimately "members." We are disciples. This is the new identity we must embrace if we are to live in the new pentecost.

A Fixed Message

Participation in God's new pentecost is an intensely spiritual experience, but it is not a vague experience. Before he ascended, Jesus told his followers that the reason they would soon be filled with the Spirit was so they could be his witnesses (Acts 1:8). This is the purpose of every pentecost. When we identify ourselves as apostles and allow the wind of the Spirit to blow into us, we understand that we are "sent" to make Christ known. Jesus is the Gospel.

We must not lose this central fact in all our other considerations. A new pentecost changes many things and challenges many things. We have already alluded to some of those things in the previous meditations. We will identify more as we move along. If we are not careful, we might think that everything is in flux. But that is not the case. We have a fixed message: Jesus is Lord. New pentecosts come upon the earth in order that this message might get out to the world in fresh ways.

In this regard, I have come to view "the Spirit-filled life" in a new way. In his farewell discourse in the upper room, Jesus spoke to the apostles about the coming of the Holy Spirit, and he said plainly, "He will glorify me" (John 16:14). In the economy of the Trinity, each Person is a means to help us see the other two better. The Father glorifies the Son, and the Son glorifies the Father. All the members of the Trinity honor all the other members, and each member shares in a common nature.

The Holy Spirit has come to glorify the Son so that both the Father and the Son may be better seen and more faithfully followed. This is a mystery, but it is also necessary for us to grasp. We are to emulate the Trinity. That is, we are to go into the world as Spirit-filled people to do what the indwelling Spirit does: glorify Christ. In this regard I have come to see that the fruit of the Spirit, which Paul identifies in Galatians 5:22–23, is the characteristic of Christ himself, and right after Paul lists the nine dimensions, he says they are evidences that we belong to Christ (Gal 5:24). The emphasis is not upon the Spirit, or upon us; the emphasis is—and remains—on Jesus. This means that no matter what kind of "pentecostal experience" we have, it is for the purpose of making Christ real in our lives and known in the world.

It is so important for us to see this and bond ourselves strongly to it. Church history contains numerous examples of people and communities who became fixated on the Holy Spirit. Everything was about the

Spirit. And everyone inside and outside the community was judged in relation to their experience of the Spirit. Preaching and teaching became concentrated on the gifts of the Spirit, the manifestations of the Spirit, the prosperity which comes to us by the Spirit, and so forth. For all practical purposes, these communities might as well have changed their name from "Christians" to "Spiritans."

New pentecosts point to the Spirit but do not center themselves in the Spirit. In true pentecosts, Jesus remains central. Our relationship is with Jesus. To be "Christian" is to be "like Christ." It is to be filled with the mind of Christ, given the heart of Christ, and sent forth to do the work of Christ. Any shift from this centrality caricatures and counterfeits pentecost. The Holy Spirit is the means to the pentecostal experience, not the end of it. Jesus is the Gospel.

We see this clearly when the 120 left the upper room and went down to the streets of Jerusalem to witness to those who had come into the city to celebrate the Feast of Pentecost. Taking his opening words from the prophet Joel, Peter immediately applied Joel's prediction to Jesus, and the rest of Peter's sermon focused squarely on Jesus (Acts 2:14-36). His invitation to the crowd was not to be filled with the Spirit, as he and the others had just been; his invitation was to repent and be baptized "in the name of Jesus Christ" (Acts 2:38). The first Christian Pentecost was rooted in Jesus, and every authentic one since has been similarly centered.

Related to this is the fact that as people come to faith in Christ, they become our brothers and sisters. Conversion and community are always united. There can never be a private, "me and Jesus" spirituality. Every new pentecost is a renewal of Christian fellowship. As some have said, the Jesus in me meets the Jesus in you, and we become members together in the Body of Christ. Just as pentecost produces "a Jesus person," it also produces "Jesus people." We will say more about this later in the book.

For now, the point is to understand that Christology is the heart and core of our faith and of the movements that arise in the world to make our faith known. If we lose the centrality and ultimacy of Jesus in our exuberance to be part of a new pentecost, we will find ourselves working against the very purposes for which the pentecost occurred in the first place. New pentecost people always live within range of Jesus' own words: "When I am lifted up from the earth, I will draw everyone to me" (John 12:32).

Abundant Living

When we understand that we are apostles sent into the world to make Christ known, we realize that the new pentecost is offering people Christ on the same terms that he offered himself to them, and with the same purpose in mind. Jesus spelled this out for us in his many words and deeds, but everything came together in his declaration, "I came that they may have life, and have it abundantly" (John 10:10). Participation in a new pentecost is both experiencing this abundant life and, in turn, offering it to others. God's new pentecost is about moving us from death to life.

This idea is embedded in the creation story (Gen 1:1–2:3). The earth was formless and empty. But the Spirit "hovered" over it, and the lifeless came alive. A desolate planet began to teem with life. The climax came when God "breathed" (spirited) into humans the "breath" (spirit) of life, and we became living souls. The creation story sets the agenda for the rest of the Bible: God is the God of Life. And we come alive as God intended when we live what some people today are calling "the with-God life."[3]

The same idea is conveyed dramatically in Ezekiel's conversation with God about the dry bones (Ezek 37). Once again, God "breathes" (spirits) on the bones, and they begin to live. It commences as a rattling. It continues as a connecting. Sinews are then added, and everything is covered with skin. But it is only when the Spirit enters into the bodies that "they live" (Ezek 37:10). This story applies directly to the nation of Israel, which had become like the dry bones. God could not be satisfied to leave them in that condition. God is the God of Life. So, when Jesus stood before the crowd and said that his aim was to give them abundant life, there was a whole biblical tradition to reveal the life-giving intention of God.

This message came to be summarized in two words: "in Christ." Jesus set the stage for it in his invitation in John 15 to abide in him. The imagery is the same; branches separated from the vine cannot live, and they cannot bear fruit. The presence and power of wind on the day of Pentecost is an infusion of life into the believers, so that they can abide in Jesus and bear fruit (remember Gal 5:22–23) in his name. As the believers scattered into the world beyond Jerusalem, their message was Christ, and their invitation was to live "in him."

---

3. I have been particularly helped in seeing the centrality of "the with-God life" by the Renovaré ministry in general and the book titled *Life With God*, by Richard Foster and Kathryn Helmers (New York: HarperOne, 2008).

One of the clearest places to see this is 2 Corinthians 5:17, where Paul wrote, "If anyone is in Christ, there is a new creation: everything old has passed away; see, everything has become new!" And from that new life there arise ministries of reconciliation that offer the same life to any who will receive it. While the passage is not specifically about Pentecost, or the work of the Spirit in our lives, it is rooted in the Jesus-centeredness that we spoke of in the last meditation. From Paul's words we discover what pentecostal life looks like.

First, we see the *essence* of abundant living. It is being "in Christ." We return to John 15 to see what this means. To be alive in Christ is to be united to him, to abide in him—to be connected with him. Look at vines and branches, Jesus said, and you will understand what it means to be "in me." When we do that we find that it is a living connection—a literal passing of life between parties. It is a natural connection—nothing forced, nothing that calls attention to itself. It is a continuous connection—not occasional or hit-and-miss. It is a fruitful connection, one that gives life rather than takes it away. And it is a joyful connection—the kind of life that causes us to exclaim, "This is what I was made for!"

Second, we see the *experience* of abundant living. It is being "a new creation." There are other words Paul could have used, and the verse would still have probably made it into the Bible. But he described life in Christ in terms of creation. In effect, he was saying, "Remember dimensions of the first creation, and you will understand what the new creation is to be." It is comprehensive—not just a partial experience. It is initially formless—not yet in the full shape God intends it to have. It is progressively developed in a "little by little" (day-by-day) fashion. It is marvelously varied—no "one size fits all" paradigm is allowed. It is intricately connected—a "system" of interrelatedness, where individual parts cannot exist in isolation from the other parts. And it is all divinely blessed.

From this transforming experience we find the *expression* of abundant living. Paul says that the "old things have gone away . . . new things have arrived." Obsolete dimensions of our life cease to exercise their control over us; obstacles are removed, so that we can have direct access to God. Life replaces death. And when that is so, we are given ministries of reconciliation that take us into the world to befriend and serve others in Jesus' name.

We see this same thing happening in the first Christian Pentecost. When the believers in the upper room were filled with the Spirit, their first move was to leave the room, go downstairs, and hit the streets. The opening manifestation of their life in Christ was ministry in the world. They did not make this move in a spirit of judgmentalism or triumphalism, but in a spirit that said, "We cannot imagine anyone, anywhere failing to miss the abundant life Jesus came to give!" This is still the purpose of a new pentecost.

No Illusions

The first Christian Pentecost created a new community, but it began as a fellowship within Judaism. The early Christians continued to worship in the Temple and to practice their faith through means largely provided to them by their Jewish heritage. In fact, Christianity only became a distinct religion further down the line when a great persecution arose against the church in Jerusalem (Acts 8:1). At the start, the first Christians didn't seem to be in any hurry to separate themselves from their parent religion. And even after they did, they took with them a large measure of their Jewish tradition—including the Hebrew Scriptures.

This is another key factor in understanding a new pentecost and living in it. When God moves in a fresh way on the earth, it is through existing communities. It is impossible to imagine how a new movement, congregation, or denomination could come into existence without any reference to a prior Christian tradition. On the contrary, new pentecosts are born within the very structures they seek to renew. Renewal comes from what has been called "little churches in the big church."

I see this principle at work in Jesus' conversation with Nicodemus regarding the new birth (John 3). Every baby born comes out of its mother. Before it does so, it spends nine months gestating in the womb. The baby is not the mother—it is a distinct human being—but it shares general human characteristics with her and with every other human being. And more specifically, even minutes after its birth, people will say that the baby has its mother's eyes or its daddy's nose. There is no birth without parents. And the Bible makes it clear that we are to honor our fathers and mothers.

I have lived long enough to watch godly friends leave existing churches and go out on their own to start new ones. I have absolutely no right to judge whether what they did was right or wrong. And I am not writing now to make any kind of evaluation of their actions. But I can make observations. And what I have observed is that the new churches usually end up looking a lot like the ones they left. Property is located, buildings constructed, budgets made and financial campaigns launched. Leaders are chosen, services conducted, programs planned and missionaries supported. The sick are visited. The dead are buried. Prayer meetings are held. And a variety of communication pieces (newsletters, e-letters, and Web sites) are developed to keep everyone on the same page.

But more than the institutional similarities, I have observed what might be called the "psychological similarities." When I am asked to speak at meetings where these pastoral leaders are in attendance, I hear them talking about the same kinds of things during break times as the traditional pastors do. They are facing the same stresses and strains, dealing with the same challenges, and taking the same hits. The name on the church sign is different, but life together inside is not all that different from what they left behind.

Again, it may sound like I am trying to say that the decision to begin something new was a mistake. In some cases, I'm sure that has turned out to be true. But that is not the point I am trying to make. I am only trying to emphasize that in a new pentecost, the new communities that are born are very similar to the older ones. The mark of a pentecostal community is not that it is "problem free." Church never ceases to be messy.

Within a very short time, the group who had been "all together in one place" (Acts 2:1) had separated into factions (the Hellenists and the Hebrews) and had begun to disagree over whether or not the widows were being taken care of properly (Acts 6:1). After Paul had made the rounds to visit the emerging churches in the Greco-Roman world, his final visit with the Ephesian elders reminded them that "savage wolves" would arise against the church, and some of them would be fellow Christians (Acts 20:30).

What does this mean? And why include a meditation like this in a book about a new pentecost? Simply to make it clear that there are no illusions. God is not calling any of us to live in a new pentecost in order to escape "the mean old church" and exist as a rarified, purified group of people. When the first monks were moved by the Spirit to "flee" the city and go into the desert, they found demons waiting for them in the wastes and caves there, much as they had in their previous locations.

God calls new communities into existence during a time of new pentecost. But it is not a call to move from evil to good or from the imperfect to the perfect. If we are going to be leaders in God's new pentecost, there must be no illusions—only commitments. We will explore this aspect of God's new community in the next meditation.

Pentecostal Community

In the history of Christianity, vital and viable communities form in relation to identifiable commitments. One principle runs through them all: experience alone is not sufficient to form or sustain the pentecostal moment. Luke makes it clear that the first three thousand believers were devoted to the Lord (Acts 2:42). But in the same verse, that devotion worked itself out into a pattern of personal and corporate behavior. Historically, this has come to be called the making and keeping of a rule of life. It is the context for this chapter as we consider the nature and practices of pentecostal community.

For us today, perhaps the most important thing we must say about a rule of life is that it has nothing to do with "legalism" or a law-keeping Christianity. We hear the word *rule* and immediately we think it means rules and regulations. But if we think that, then it's a short step to a faith that is really punitive in its structure and application—that is, "do this or else." But the fact is, when the phrase "rule of life" came to be the description of life together, the word *rule* was being used in relation to its Latin meaning of "trellis"—a structure to keep flowers from growing wildly in a garden.

When I learned this one fact, my entire understanding of a rule of life changed, and it became something that I actually wanted. I had been a Christian long enough to know that my impulses could take me in all sorts of directions—not all of them bad, by any means—just "all over the map." I knew what it felt like to be "three miles wide and a half inch deep." I knew what superficial Christianity was, and I didn't believe it was what Christ had in mind for his followers. I had come to see that busyness and blessedness are not the same thing, that stress is not the key evidence of sanctification.

Thus, I sort of "backed into" my understanding of the value and place of a rule of life. I came to know that John Wesley began the Methodist movement with the United Societies and that they were ordered by the "General Rules." It was some years later that I realized that Wesley was consciously developing Methodism as a kind of "third order" within Anglicanism—much like many others in Roman Catholicism had done and continue to do today. I learned that he could not come right out and say this, or he would have been labeled a "papist" and shunned. So, he just kept quiet about the practice and developed the third-order principle in early Methodist life together. When I found this out, it made me want to know more about living by rule.

I turned to the Rule of St. Benedict and to the Rule of St. Francis. These have been the foci of my ongoing study, with related side trips into other expressions both ancient and modern. All this has been so fascinating for me that I have come to believe John Wesley was consciously drawing on both rules and saints in his development of early Methodism. But that is a subject for another book! For now, the point is simply that a pentecostal community cannot be sustained on the basis of experience alone; it requires a "rule of life." I believe Acts 2:42–47 is the rule for the first Christian community in Jerusalem. Let's look at it briefly.

First, they developed their internal life through four means: the apostles' teaching (instruction), fellowship (support, encouragement, and accountability), the breaking of bread (probably both the Lord's Supper and socializing), and the prayers (notice the use of the plural, probably indicating that they observed the stated hours of prayer in Judaism). We must pause and see how each of these things was necessary for long-term existence.

There must be instruction. Knowledge can never be separated from vital piety. A devotional life without doctrine—or doctrine without devotional life—results in a diminishment of both. Faith is always "taught," and especially so after the first generation of any movement dies out. There is no virtue in wasting time trying to decide whether knowledge or piety is more important; they are equal in significance, just as inhaling and exhaling are equally part of breathing.

There must be supportive community. Going out into the world in Jesus' name raises all sorts of questions and creates challenging pressures. We must have some place to go to be encouraged, counseled, and forgiven. Satan can "pick us off" one at a time (and often does), but as the writer of Ecclesiastes knew, a cord made up of several strands is not so easily broken (4:12). Formation and fellowship can never be separated. Life in Christ is always life together. It is no accident that Dietrich Bonhoeffer created the pattern of a "day apart" and a "day together" in the community he led.

There must also be a sacramental and social core. In fact, I personally believe that it is a good thing not to isolate the Lord's Supper from the idea of a meal together. I'm glad that New Testament scholars do not know for sure what "breaking of bread" means; it probably means both. The first Christians ate and drank "in remembrance" of Jesus. Even if they had a formal service of Eucharist, it didn't contain all the aspects of our services today. I like to think that they lived together in such a way that even when they sat down to eat together in their homes, they believed Jesus was with them—and at the center—as much as anywhere else. We can include a full-blown theology of the Lord's Supper here as we like, but hopefully, not in a way that makes a dining table in a home separate from a communion table in a church.

And, finally, there must be prayers. We will look at this in more detail later in the book, but for now let me simply say that stated times of prayer are one of the best ways to train ourselves in a life of prayer. I grew up in a morning-devotional, quiet-time-oriented Christianity. It is still the mainstay of my spiritual formation. But thankfully, I came to see that it was intended to be only one of a number of "calls to prayer" and devotion during the day. Numerous models and means have arisen throughout Christianity, and in principle no one is better than another. The aim is to live a devotional life, not just to have a devotional time. By the use of the word *prayers* in the text, we can see that from the start the first Christians didn't think of any single "time" as containing the full content of their praying.

Here are the fundamental expressions of the internal rule of life for the first Christians. But Luke does not stop here. A gaining of the "mind of Christ" is also a taking on of the heart and work of Christ. In Acts 2:43–47, the faith of the first disciples hits the streets. Their rule of life becomes not simply communal, but missional. Before the sun has barely set on the first Christian Pentecost, the Bible clearly shows that holiness must be social as well as personal. The world is our parish.

It began with "signs and wonders." Some people would like to skip over this and go straight to more traditional social action dimensions of their life together. But we cannot get to verse 44 without engaging with verse 43. Living in God's new pentecost forces all of us to ask what it means to be a community where signs and wonders are exhibited. And when it comes to that, I think the important thing is not to try to define the form of signs and wonders but to insure the authenticity of them.

I have known communities where there "had to be" signs and wonders. And when there were not, they were "manufactured" anyway. I remember attending a service where there had been no outward manifestation of tongues. Because this was a defining sign for the community, the pastor could not dismiss the service without some kind of "tongue" being spoken. So, he led us in an exercise where we were told to talk out loud "faster and faster," saying whatever word came to mind; at some point English would evolve into glossolalia. Well, I have to admit that the congregation's noise evolved into something, but I am pretty sure it was not the gift of tongues. Whatever else "signs and wonders" means, it means that they happen *to* us, not because of us! But this does mean that a pentecostal community is one that is open to whatever God chooses to do in its midst.

At the same time, let's be clear that this does not always have to be something "abnormal" or "unusual." One of the signs of a pentecostal community is its commitment to ordinary holiness, as its members go out into the world to live as faithful witnesses, not secret disciples. One of the wonders of a pentecostal community is its willingness to live in ways that tell the world, "It's not about us." Just as we err when we try to create signs and wonders, so do we err when we believe that they always have to be "spectacular" to be real.

And that leads us right into the rest of the section. The believers did not consider their possessions to be their exclusive property. The members of the Jerusalem community sold their possessions and goods and distributed the proceeds to any and all who were in need, both inside their fellowship and beyond it. It is important to note that we do not see this specific practice mentioned again in any of the other churches, so that what we take from this section is not a one-size-fits-all practice or requirement, but a spirit that recognizes that we do not live for ourselves only but for the well-being of others. A pentecostal community will practice specific acts of mercy and service, but the precise forms will vary from one place to another.

Here is one of the places where I think we can differentiate institutional Christianity from pentecostal community. In too many congregations there is nothing that binds us together between Sundays. We come into a sanctuary, sit in our customary pews, worship with those who have decided to show up along with us, and then we leave, never to see or be seen again until the following Sunday (if then). We have no rule of life to guide us, no pattern that calls us to remain connected and mindful of one another. Without a rule of life, we just come and go in a kind of randomized spirituality that doubtless does much good, but not as much good as a community that lives with a holy trellis to keep its members from becoming wildflowers in the Kingdom.

TWO
A New Monasticism

A New Monasticism

The previous meditations have been intended to lead us into an awareness of the reality and essence of a new pentecost. There is always more that could be said about a particular subject, but hopefully these meditations are enough to establish that we are living in a time when a fresh wind of God's Spirit is blowing, and that God is inviting us to become part of the experience. The question now becomes, what kind of person must we be to be involved in a new pentecost? I choose to answer the question by saying, "We must be *monks*."

For many of us, this will take some getting used to. We did not grow up in an ecclesiology where monks were part of the picture. We may have even grown up in traditions where people who lived the monastic life were considered "weird"—and, in a few cases, viewed as living lives antithetical to the Gospel itself. As we move into the second segment of this book, we must not think that defining life in a new pentecost as *monastic* will be easy for everyone to accept, much less live into. But I am going to stick with the one-word answer and hope that the remainder of the meditations in this section will at least tell you why I have chosen the word, and perhaps even serve to attract you to a new way of living in Christ.

My justification in using the word *monk* to describe the person living in a new pentecost comes from the basic meaning of the word: "singular" or "alone." This is the meaning of the Greek word *monos*. At first glance, the two definitions seem to be describing the same thing, and to be sure, there is an overlap between them. But for the purposes of this book, it is helpful to show through each word a distinctive element of living in God's new pentecost.

First, to be a monk is to be *singular*. To be a monk is to be a person who has staked his or her life on three words: "Jesus is Lord." He is not one among several or many lords, but exclusively and supremely Lord. Singularity conveys the notion of ultimacy. Jesus is Lord. He has no rivals, and there is none higher than he. It is likely that this was the first creed of the earliest Christians. The phrase itself appears in the text of the New Testament, and it continued to be a central affirmation thereafter. To be a monk is to be a person who lives a singular life based upon a central affirmation.

We often hear people say that Christianity must be counter-cultural. But we do not always realize that saying "Jesus is Lord" is the most counter-cultural aspect of our faith. It is the statement from which all other counter-cultural attitudes and actions flow. It was a controversial statement when the first Christians made it, and it continues to be so to this day. The world is not prepared to think in categories that force choices. We want everyone to be "pretty good" and almost every way of life (except the most horrendous) to be "good enough." But when we say that Jesus is Lord, we have called every non-Jesus way into question. Can you think of any way of life more counter-cultural than that?

But rather than taking the affirmation immediately to the world and using it as a prism through which to see other ways of living, we must first apply it to ourselves. To say "Jesus is Lord" is to slay the ego. It is not to set up a soul-wearying list of laws, but rather to declare that the old self has died (Rom 6:6). Our self-centered, self-referential, self-reliant "self" (false self) no longer lives. Egotism has come to an end. Paul said the same thing in Galatians 2:20. Let me write it out for you exactly like the original Greek says it: "I am living no longer as an 'I,' but in me Christ lives."

It took me years to see the meaning of this verse, the challenge of this verse, and even the scandal of this verse. I no longer live as an "I." The Greek word for "I" is *ego*. Egotism is over. I no longer live in a world of self-exalted, competitive egos, each of which tries to have its way and will do whatever it takes to "win." The radical nature of Christianity is its singularity—Jesus is Lord. It is no longer about having or getting my way; it is now about living so that God's will is done on earth as it is in heaven.

Before leaving singularity behind, one related point needs to be made. To say that the ego dies does not mean that the person God intended me to be dies also. That's why the Christian faith differentiates between the false self (ego) and the true self (soul). God has made each of us to be holy. God would never destroy that. But God is against everything that seeks to turn "soul" into "ego." So, to declare that Jesus is Lord is to confess to ourselves and to the world that we want to live as human beings made in the image of God and redeemed by Christ to experience abundant life. This means we are *monks*—men and women who live with singular devotion to Jesus.

Second, to be a monk is to be *alone*. For some in Christian history this has taken the form of living as a hermit. But every monk knows that the word *alone* is not limited to the form it takes. To be "alone" is to be abandoned to God. This is the idea of surrender. This picks up where singularity leaves off, telling us that the goal of the Spirit-filled life is not the annihilation of the self, but the consecration of it—not the cancellation of our selves, but the consecration of our selves (see Rom 12:1).

The amazing thing about abandonment is that it puts us squarely into the picture of our own deliverance from evil. John Wesley said it simply: "Without God, we cannot; without us, God will not." *Abandonment* is the fundamental term to describe what the Bible means when it tells us to work out our salvation with fear and trembling (Phil 2:12). Abandonment is the engagement of the will in ways that enables us to respond to the grace freely given to us by God in Christ. Abandonment is our "yes" spoken in response to God's prior "yes" in Jesus.

This all came together for me in a beautiful way the first time I visited the Abbey of Gethsemani in Kentucky. As I entered into the guesthouse, I passed under the door facing. On it were these words, etched in stone: *God Alone*. I had an intuitive sense of their meaning. But I had a very unformed historic sense of the words—surely an incomplete sense of why the Cistercian Order would choose to put those words over the doorway into their guesthouse. Over time, that has all changed. The historicity of the words has met with my own personal experience of them.

And this is why I say that the kind of person who lives in a new pentecost is a *monk*—one who lives with affirmation and abandonment, with singularity and surrender. And why does this matter? Simply because most of us live for a long time (even as Christians) with a "God + _____" spirituality. Oh, we want God, but we want God for all sorts of personal, communal, economic, and political reasons. So, our life and our faith become a "God + _____" experience. Each of us fills in the blank with all sorts of secondary words. But we design a life where it is always "God + _____."

A monk in a new pentecost lives with a "God Alone" commitment. A monk in a new pentecost is singular and surrendered. He or she wants to be an incarnation of Jesus' admonition to "seek first the Kingdom of God and his righteousness, and all these other things will be added unto you" (Matt 6:33). To be a monk in a new pentecost is to live in paradox, where in having nothing, one ends up possessing all things (2 Cor 6:10). This is life in Christ. This is salvation. This is joy!

Domestic Monks

When a new pentecost occurs, traditional monasticism usually increases. Men and women feel a call from God to become members of an established community. If God should call you to that kind of life, I would urge you to visit a monastery or convent near where you live and learn more about it. Even if you do not choose the life of a traditional monk, I believe you will still find periodic visits to cloistered communities to be of great benefit.

But in our day, God is raising up a new kind of monk—a domestic monk. This is a person who remains in the world but who lives with the kind of singularity and surrender we looked at in the last meditation. This is God's call in a new pentecost, and it is one that every disciple should respond to in one way or another. The response may be an affiliation with a traditional monastic community as an oblate member. Or it may be to join with others in the growing phenomenon called "the new monasticism."

I first saw the principle of domestic monasticism as I was studying Jesus' call to the first disciples: "Come follow me, and I will show you how to fish for people" (Mark 1:17). One day I realized that Jesus was speaking to fishermen. His call was rooted in what they already knew. It was an invitation to take their current knowledge and invest it in the Kingdom of God. This completely altered the way I saw discipleship, and it has reframed my understanding of ministry.

Fishermen know how to fish. So, Jesus was saying, "Take what you know about fishing and imagine doing those same things for my sake." I have come to believe this is one of the most transforming things Jesus ever said. But I am not a fisherman. So, I began to talk about this with people who like to fish. I asked them to ponder the connections between fishing for fish and fishing for people. They responded with rapid-fire suggestions: go where the fish are, be patient, have a relaxed spirit, be willing to experiment, find a good location, select the appropriate bait, and be satisfied "just to fish," even if you don't catch anything. These were the kinds of things they thought of, and it was easy to see how each principle could become part of Christian discipleship.

From there, I went on to imagine what Jesus' invitation to discipleship might sound like to other kinds of people. To doctors Jesus might say, "Follow me, and I will teach you how to cure the souls of people, as well as their bodies." To lawyers he might say, "Follow me, and I will show you how to defend those who have no advocates." To a homemaker he might say, "Follow me, and I will teach you how to care for people inside your family unit." To a football coach he might say, "Follow me, and I will show you how to have a winning team in the Kingdom."

Jesus' invitation to Christian discipleship is extended to every one of us, and it begins within the context of what we already know. I've found that this is a new way of looking at things for many people. Too often we have said, "Sign up for discipleship classes," as if becoming a disciple were like learning a foreign language or a new skill. But Jesus took another approach. He began with what people already knew and used their inherent knowledge as the bridge to lead them into what I have come to call "achievable discipleship."

This is domestic monasticism. It is taking what you already know and what you already do, and doing it *for* Jesus. It is doing it *with* Jesus. Most of all, it is doing it *by* Jesus—in the power that he provides. I can only invite you to consider who you are, where you live, and what you do. Think about the routines of your life and then prayerfully ask, "Lord, what are the transferrable concepts? What are the things that I already know that I can use in your service?" Your discipleship begins by doing the things you would normally do for yourself or for your boss, and doing them for God. When you do this, you are a domestic monk—you are a person who surrenders your life to God, to be used in the singular way that you have already offered your life to be used day after day. Your discipleship may change as time goes by, but it will begin in ways you are already familiar with.

Not long ago, I was speaking to a men's group about this. After the meeting, an attorney stayed to talk to me. "I've been a member of this church since I was twelve, and I have been an attorney in this city for about twenty-five years," he said. "Tonight is the first time I've ever connected those two things." Well, thanks be to God! I could tell by the look in his eyes that a new light had come on. He was taking what he already knew and imagining how those same attitudes and actions could be invested in the Kingdom. Every one of us has the capacity to do this; we just have to stop, look, and listen. We just have to hear Jesus' call to us to hand over to him who we already are, what we already know, and what we already do. That's what it means to "follow" him.

To be a domestic monk is to live consciously as a disciple in the world every day. And as in traditional monastic life, it is also to be part of a community where this commitment can find expression in worship, study, encouragement, and support. The models for "life together" vary widely. They exist in both Roman Catholic and Protestant communities. All the expressions are illustrations of what the earliest monks discovered: that they were able to live more devoted lives when they did so in association with other monks. Even hermits were connected to some kind of community. The singularity and surrender of being a monk is not to be equated with isolation, privatization, or independence. Whether traditional or domestic, monks find that their life in Christ must have a communal dimension.

There is really nothing new under the sun. The term *domestic monk* is really a contemporary way of describing the older principle of "the priesthood of all believers." We have damaged the Body of Christ by creating fixed categories of clergy and laity, and in doing so we speak the lie of "full-time Christian service" as limited to what the clergy do. But the fact is that there is no other kind of Christian service but full time. We have spoken about "going into the ministry" as something preachers and other religious professionals do. But every believer is a minister, because every member is a disciple. To speak about being a domestic monk is to recover the general ministry of all believers and to connect that commitment to the myriad ways it can take place in the world every day.

I believe your heart will leap up and skip like a deer when you can look into a mirror and exclaim, "I am a monk for Jesus!"

Disposition of the Heart

Those who live in God's new pentecost understand that Christianity is more a disposition of the heart than it is a list of rules and regulations. They recognize that Christianity is a living faith, not a dead orthodoxy. This does not eliminate or even minimize the role of doctrine, belief, and instruction. But it means that when these things are in their proper place and have their proper content, the outcome will be a life that honors God and attracts the attention of other people.

One of my favorite phrases is "incline your hearts to the Lord." You find it occasionally in the Bible. I can visualize it. It's like lifting up our outstretched arms to God. When our hearts are inclined to Him, God can bring whatever He wishes into our lives. Our hearts are disposed to receive what God wants to give us. This disposition has been historically described in three words: faith, hope, and love.

We are people of *faith*. We are disposed to believe. I have lived the entirety of my Christian life during a time when many scholars in the church and academy taught what has been called a "hermeneutic of suspicion." They told us more about what verses were allegedly *not* in the original manuscripts of the Bible than they told us about the verses that remained. They were more certain about who did *not* write portions of the Bible than about who did. Some were even quick to assert that passages and ideas had been inserted by the church to feather its own nest and promote its own agendas, thus making the early Christians a band of manipulators. In short, these so-called scholars have said it is very difficult to "really know" what is true.

In the last thirty years or so, the number of these experts has increased, as has their boldness. I have concluded that they are, for the most part, working against the new pentecost. Many of them have knowingly departed from fundamental tenets of the Christian faith. They do not believe the historic Christian faith and are consciously at work to undermine it. In some ways, they are actually heretics. Let me be clear. I am not calling these folks "mean." Many of them are quite likeable, and a few are interesting and help me think about matters of faith. But their disposition is toward *disbelief* more than it is toward belief. And that disposition is antithetical to the ways of a new pentecost.

To say that people in a new pentecost are disposed to faith is to state that the essential content of the Christian faith has been established, and anyone who wants to can know what that content is. The Greek word for it is *kerygma*, and the first Christians made it their business to preach and teach the message. They did not believe they were free to invent the gospel, but only to proclaim it as it had been given to them. That is what a disposition toward belief creates. Furthermore, the church responded to historical and cultural challenges and developed major statements of faith called creeds. These have further served to give specificity to the word *faith*. Disciples in a new pentecost are committed to the faith that has been revealed and delivered.

But at this stage of the meditation it is important to note that the disposition toward faith is not narrow or sectarian. Disciples in a new pentecost are ecumenical. They affirm the creeds of the faith without having to add subcategories that risk dividing Christians from each other. For example, we believe that Jesus was born of a virgin, but we do not try to say precisely how that happened. We declare that Jesus was crucified for our sins, but we do not hold to only one doctrine of the atonement. We affirm that Jesus came out of the tomb alive, but we do not go on to require a specific theory of resurrection. In other words, we are people who can hold belief and mystery together in a way that does not diminish either. The goal of a new pentecost is not doctrinal conformity, but devout confession.

In doing so, we find ourselves in fellowship with Christians from traditions beyond the one we have chosen as our primary expression of the faith. One of the most exciting things that has happened to me in the last thirty years is to hold tightly to "the faith once delivered to the saints," and then discover how many other Protestants, Roman Catholics, and Orthodox brothers and sisters do also. The disposition toward faith finds us "leaning toward" many others who are also leaning toward us—because all of us are seeking to lean toward the Center, who is Christ.

And then, we are disposed to *hope*. Like the writer of Hebrews we do not see all things in subjection to God (2:8). Every day we see many people, places, and things that do not reflect the will of God. We see people living as victimizers, or as victims. We see the results of natural disasters and human diseases that point toward the creation's fallenness. We do not see the world the way God intends for it to be, but we do see Jesus (Heb 2:9). We live with hope. We do not believe that any evil person, place, or thing has "the last word." We believe that Jesus is the Word (John 1:1, 14) and that he will have the final say over everything.

You do not have to be a Christian to know how essential hope is. Professionals in the behavioral sciences can cite example after example of the difference hope makes in the lives of people. In fact, we know that in everything hope is better than fatalism. As Christians, we simply say, "Why not put our hope in its ultimate place—in Christ?" If I live by hope, then not only do I want to have hope; I also want to put that hope in the highest and best place. And that "place" is a Person—Jesus Christ. He is my hope. My disposition toward hope is a disposition toward him.

There are people today who see this as artificial and naïve. But we must remember that hope is also related to a sense of eternity. It is a terrible thing for a mother and father to hold their baby only for a few minutes after birth. Every baby is intended to live a lot longer than that. But we have hope, because we do not "measure" the length or quality of life in terms of years spent on the earth. Every person who lives, lives forever. Every human being lives on the earth for a different length of time; there is no "ideal" length of earthly life. Even when a person's life is cut short by all reasonable estimates, we do not call that "the end." We have hope that the God we know in Jesus Christ receives the souls of the departed and they remain alive forevermore. We are disposed to be people of hope, because we are disposed to believe in Jesus and to see him in the context of eternity.

And finally, we are disposed to *love*. That love is rooted in the nature of God (*agape*) and given to us through the Holy Spirit. It is defined and manifested in relation to the two great commandments: to love God with all our heart, soul, mind, and strength, and to love our neighbors as we love ourselves. It is a love that calls for totality ("all") and universality ("everyone"). Most of the love we experience and share is partial, conditional, and limited. It is the nature of love (*agape*) that makes Christianity different, and it is the giving of that love to us through grace that makes living a life of love (*agape*) possible in the first place.

Our disposition to love begins "within reach" and is extended to the people we know and live with every day. It comes through what we typically call "time, talent, and treasure." But we then go on to test the reality of our love through decisions we make to be instruments of love beyond our ability to be in personal relationships. This is love defined as stewardship. We see the resources God has given us as means to share love with people—many of whom we will never even meet. Once again, our time, talent, and treasure is available to be used as God leads. As someone has said it, "We live simply, so that others may simply live."

The transforming nature of *agape* must not be missed. It is important for us to recognize what kind of love this is and what it means to say that our hearts are disposed to love. In Greek there are four words for love: *phileo, eros, storge,* and *agape.* The first three are in some ways dependent upon the response of the one being loved. So, if a person receives our love (*phileo, eros,* and *storge*), we are inclined to give more love. If not, we're tempted to reduce it. These three loves fluctuate. The fourth love—*agape*—is different. It is love that is defined by the one doing the loving. It is not given or withheld in relation to the response. A person may accept or reject *agape*, but we love anyway. A person may receive *agape* or rebel against it, but we love anyway.

As I have thought about this and shared it with others, the response often is, "Who could ever love like that?" And the answer is, "No one but God." And that's why the Bible says that "*the love of God* has been poured out in our hearts through the Holy Spirit" (Rom 5:5). Our disposition toward love is a disposition toward a kind of love that can only exist when God is alive in us.

When we live in a new pentecost, we live in it as people who have inclined our hearts to the Lord. We are people disposed toward faith, hope, and love. We dare to believe that these three qualities of life are what millions of people are lacking, yet long for. And we dare to believe that God has put us on the earth to be recipients of these things and to be instruments through whom others can have them as well.

Dimensions of the Life

Faith, hope, and love do not "hang in the air" in an intangible way. The spiritual life has identifiable dimensions through which it is mediated. The three ways often talked about in spiritual formation literature are body, soul, and spirit. I'll use the next segment of meditations to introduce these dimensions and show how they are the means God is using to invite us to live in a new pentecost. I'll begin with a meditation that looks at these three dimensions as a whole.

In the history of Christian spirituality one of the great dangers was (and is) dualism—not only a separation of body and spirit, but also an elevation of spirit over body. Over the centuries various groups have been dualistic in their understanding and practice of the spiritual life. It is not necessary to examine history in order to confront this fallacy. But it is important to point out that we are not immune to the same problem today.

It was a wonderful day in my spiritual formation when I learned that the word *salvation* means "wholeness." It does not simply mean going to heaven when we die. The God who wills eternal life for us also wills abundant life (John 10:10) and seeks to establish and promote it in every dimension of our being. So, about thirty years after Jesus ascended into heaven, Paul came along and wrote that God wants to sanctify our spirits, souls, and bodies (1 Thess 5:23). From that time onward, we have been trying to discover more of what the Bible was pointing us toward in that phrase.

Taken as a whole, it means that God is interested in every part of our creation—every part of what it means to be "human." Similarly, in the new creation (2 Cor 5:17), God wants a whole-life transformation. We have already been pointing toward a whole-life spirituality in previous meditations. For example, God is as interested in our living a Kingdom-oriented life in our regular, everyday activities as He is in our doing so at church. There is no separation. In fact, our identity as disciples demands that we come to understand this and live accordingly. To speak of living in a new pentecost as human beings—body, soul, and spirit—is to say that God wants us to live with the entirety of our humanity available and engaged.

I have been saying for a while now that the next time we revise the hymnal in my denomination, I hope that "The Hokey Pokey" will be added. For one thing, most folks know it, having sung it since they were children. But more than that, I like the progression. The song begins with our putting our "left foot in." And then, as you know, it builds stanza by stanza until in the final verse we put our "whole self in." And not only that, we "shake it all about." And at the end we exclaim, "That's what it's all about!"

Indeed! Living in God's new pentecost is putting our whole self in and shaking it about. St. Benedict referred to it as offering the totality of our lives to Christ. The single word for doing this is *heart*. The heart stands for not only the deepest part of our lives, but also the widest. It stands for not only particular dimensions that we can talk about, but also for the comprehensive offering of anything and everything to God.

As I have begun to talk with people about this kind of spirituality, I have found that it is both exciting and liberating. It's exciting because every person can imagine himself or herself as one of God's beloved servants.

This cuts against the grain of the heresy of "celebrity Christianity" where only the brightest and best, the winners, are desired and used by God. It is liberating because it means that we can offer our true selves to God, not a caricature of some other believer. Our spiritual life is not one that is valid when it looks like someone else's, but when it "shines" with the radiance of our created uniqueness. When we put our whole self in, we discover that God takes our lives and uses them in ways that most often seem "natural." That's why God's people will often tell you, "It's nothing." It really doesn't feel like we are doing all that much, when the fact is that we are doing exactly what God put us on the earth to do.

A seventeenth-century writer, Jean-Pierre de Caussade, took the big word *holiness* and defined it this way: Doing the next thing you have to do, and doing it for God. You mean that's it? That's holiness? De Caussade would smile and say, "Yes, that's it!" And it is a *big* it, a divine it—God's "it" for you. This vision does not mean God's will remains static throughout the years of our lives, because our lives are evolving and developing. But because we are moving with God, the new dimensions of our discipleship will feel more like taking steps than taking leaps.

In Acts 17:28 Luke wrote that it is in God that we live, move, and have our being. Other than the word *God*, the most important word in the verse is *we*. It is essential that *we* live, move, and have our being in God. The "we" is the authentic and whole self, consecrated to God (which is what living "in" God means) and allowing the wind of the Spirit to blow into and through us for whatever purposes bring glory to God. The dimensions through which the Spirit moves are body, soul, and spirit. The context is community. God is saying to each of us, "Put your whole self in." We turn now to the three specifics of what that means.

Body

We are in desperate need of a truly Christian spirituality of the body. We live in a time when the body is grossly misunderstood, most often through pornographic images and self-gratifying attempts to glorify the flesh. In either case, we end up with a counterfeit concept of "body." This is tragic in itself, but especially because the Christian faith has a sacred place for the body, including the incarnation of the Son of God. In God's new pentecost, there is a "body" dimension to spiritual life.

I have found St Francis' understanding of the body to be helpful. He said that his body was his "cell." Far from thinking of his body as a prison, he thought of it in the original meaning of the word *cell*, as celestial—a place where heaven and earth come together. With respect to the body, we have no better overarching understanding than this: the body is a temple of the Holy Spirit (1 Cor 6:19). There is nothing we can say more important about our bodies in relation to a new pentecost, because it is precisely in the body where the Spirit wants to dwell, and it is through our bodies that the Spirit wants to work.

To think of our bodies as temples is to think of them as sacred. Anything that diminishes our physicality or distorts the meaning of body is evil—a perversion of the very "place" where a new pentecost exists and manifests itself. There are so many ways in which this happens today that we cannot even begin to list them in a single meditation, much less describe them in any detail. We face no greater challenge than to recover the idea that our bodies are holy, and that as temples they are the "houses of worship" where God is acknowledged and glorified.

We must now ask how this is done. A concept without a corresponding plan of implementation goes nowhere. It is essential to declare the sacredness of the body, but how do we go about actually making our bodies sacred? We must not ignore any valid means of doing this, and for some of us, it will mean caring for our bodies through proper sleep, good nutrition, and regular exercise. It will mean having an annual physical so that our blood pressure and cholesterol remain manageable. All of the factors that help us maintain healthy bodies will be part of the picture.

The history of Christian spirituality shows a proper concern for the body. We sometimes think of monks as extremists, but their favorite word was *moderation*. They took care to sleep, eat, and work in accordance with life-giving patterns. Unfortunately, we forget this by concentrating on some ascetics who did go to extremes, or who were called to a season of intense deprivation. But when we step back and look at the whole, we find our earliest mothers and fathers taking good care of themselves. Examples of this are included in the Rule of St. Benedict. Later, St. Francis of Assisi put it into words by saying that the soul rides on the back of Brother Donkey, reminding us that if our body breaks down, that's as far as the soul will go.

So, we begin our practice of "body" spirituality with the exhortation to keep our bodies in good shape. We then proceed to certain devotional practices that will not only enable us to do this, but also to be the living sacrifices we are called to be. We begin with solitude. Our predecessors believed that we would never live the life God intended for us if we did not remove ourselves from the noise and clamor of the world. The voices of a fallen world—to say nothing of the principalities and powers—are the very ones that lead us to a pornographic or otherwise damaged view of the body. We must come out of the world in order to see how deceptive it is. We must come out of the world in order to hear God's Voice speaking a singular word of direction to us. That happens in solitude.

Solitude is not ultimately being by ourselves, although there is an important form of solitude in which we dwell with God directly and without any distractions. But we also find the early Christians practicing solitude together, because solitude is more about creating "sacred space" than it is about being alone. In fact, Jesus invited the apostles to experience solitude as a group (Mark 6:31). The word used to describe the monk's place of solitude was *cell*, which does not mean a limited space so much as "a little piece of heaven."

The call to solitude may be the most challenging aspect of living in God's new pentecost, because we no longer live in a world that provides or values solitude. We are bombarded by sights and sounds, and we have the capacity to connect with them at any moment of the day. Electric lighting has caused us to lose the natural rhythms of day and night, the cycle of being awake and being asleep. As a result, we are a sleep-deprived and overstimulated people. Both of these conditions undermine solitude.

A while back I happened to be listening to National Public Radio when one of the pioneers of computer technology was being interviewed. He spoke of how he formerly went around the country telling people how to use the new technology, which, in the early days, he saw as an avenue for opening us to life. Now, he said, the first thing he teaches people is where the off switch is. He has come to view our fascination with technology and our incessant use of it as detrimental to life. An unchecked involvement with "everything out there" destroys solitude. And without solitude, we cannot live.

This has direct implications for living in God's new pentecost. I know pastors who act as if busyness and spirituality are the same thing. Some churches even pride themselves on being "24/7 churches." This is wrong. It is a caricature and a counterfeit. It is a religious violation of solitude. There must be a time and place for individuals and congregations to move away from the "voices" in order to hear the Voice. Thomas Merton got it right when he said that activism is a form of violence. Solitude is the call to pull the plug on our feverish rounds of unending activity—our ways of making gods out of what *we* do, so that we don't have to pay attention to what God is doing.

In our times of solitude we move into silence and stillness. In fact, solitude is the environment within which we can be silent and still. Both silence and stillness are paradoxes. We enter into silence in order to hear the Sound. Silence is the Voice of God heard by the ear of solitude. We become still in order to know how to Move. God is the source of both—the Voice and the Mover. But what follows from holy silence and stillness is different from other sounds and actions. What follows is the result of being directed by the Spirit, rather than being driven by our circumstances, passions, or dysfunctions.

We are looking at solitude, silence, and stillness in relation to the body. For each of these things requires us to make some shift in the way we use our physical capacities. Solitude calls us to move away from the "crowds." Silence calls us to shut out all the other sounds and turn off all the machines that fill us with "noise." Stillness calls us to breathe deeply, relax, and literally feel the stress within us diminishing. Each of these things is very physical, and that's why the spiritual life can never be separated from the physical life.

There was a time in my life when the word *contemplative* was not very attractive. I associated it with being detached, esoteric, and maybe even weird. It took a focused and prolonged exposure to the early desert mothers and fathers to come to a proper understanding of what it means to be contemplative. Along the way to this transformed understanding, I did meet some extremists, but the greater example came through men and women whose feet were firmly planted on the earth as they sought to lift their hearts to God.

The word *contemplate* literally means "with the template" (*con templatio*). Our template is not the world; it is Christ. He is the Template. Authentic spiritual life is being "with" him. Solitude, silence, and stillness lead us into the presence of the Risen Christ. Without solitude we may confuse Jesus with all the false messiahs put forward today. Without silence, Jesus' voice may get lost in the din of all the other voices trying to get our attention. Without stillness, our lives will move so fast that even if we do see Jesus, he will be a blur. So, for many of us, the first step toward living in God's new pentecost will be dealing with our bodies—our physicality, moving from a frenetic pace to the pace of grace.

Solitude, silence, and stillness are our companions in this aspect of the journey. Solitude gives us the space we need to be formed by the Spirit. Silence enables us to hear what the Spirit wants to say. Stillness enables us to differentiate between the movement of the Spirit and our own self-generated activism. Taken together, they engage the body in spiritual formation.

Soul

When it comes to soul, we are dealing with a dimension of the spiritual life that can be very complicated. Before Christianity even existed, there were philosophical writings on the nature and activity of the soul. There continue to be similar works in our day. There's no way to describe all that has been said about the soul. Essentially, the soul came to be viewed as the place where the body and spirit converge to produce life. The Genesis text simply says that God breathed (spirited) into the dust (body) and it became a "living soul" (2:7).

I believe that this union of body and spirit is what makes us human. We are not pure spirits, and we are not merely physical bodies. There is "something else" about us, something that enlivens us and animates our thoughts, words, and deeds. With the animals we share certain physical characteristics. With God we share certain divine characteristics. It is only when the two aspects come together that we can be described as "souls"—as human beings. E. Stanley Jones put it this way: The body without a spirit would be a corpse, but the spirit without a body would be a ghost. It takes body and spirit united to be a person.

I find this description helpful in understanding something of what it means to be human, but I must still go in search of other ideas to help me know where and how my humanity fits into my spiritual life. I return to the words of St. Francis of Assisi, when he wrote that his body was his cell. He went on to say that his soul was the hermit within. We used the idea of "cell" to describe the body's contribution to the spiritual life—the place where solitude, silence, and stillness can be practiced. Now, we add the image of the soul as the hermit within as a way to consider how we live in God's pentecost in ways that make us fully human. We will speak of that life by using the three classic elements of poverty, chastity, and obedience. These came to be related to vows in monastic communities, but prior to that they were three ways the early Christians "lived" their discipleship. If we think of the soul as that which "empowers" us to live the Christian life, we can see the importance of poverty, chastity, and obedience.

Poverty is living with an abandoned soul. We tend to define poverty in purely economic terms, but Jesus defined it in a much broader way. He did so in the first Beatitude, where he said that those who live blessed lives are those who are "poor in spirit" (Matt 5:3). Notice that the word *spirit* is not capitalized. It is not a reference to the Holy Spirit, but rather a reference to the human spirit. So, what does it mean for us to be "poor in spirit"? It means that we have emptied ourselves of all notions that we can live authentic lives without God. It means that we have abandoned any and all efforts at self-salvation. We have become "impoverished" with respect to egotism, and we have replaced it with a complete dependency upon God.

This abandonment is not limited to merely "spiritual" things; it becomes a pervasive perspective that affects and transforms every other area of life. It is a radical simplicity that will have economic ramifications as we "dematerialize" our lives through limited acquisition and generous donation. Poverty means that we move closer and closer to our needs (knowing that God wants to meet them) and further and further away from our wants (which are ways we prevent others from having what they need). Poverty is the way we become and remain humble.

Chastity is living with a faithful soul. Chastity follows poverty. It deals with more than sex. It means fidelity to the abandonment we have made. So, if we have committed ourselves to being radically dependent upon God, then the first place chastity kicks in is in helping us remain "poor in spirit." But chastity is also the guardian of all our physical appetites and desires. It is the virtue that maintains all our relationships in the condition that glorifies and pleases God. The earliest Christians knew that this did, indeed, have to do with lust and related sexual sins. But they knew that it also kept other forms of greed in check. Chastity is an aspect of soul that we need to recover in our day as greed raises its evil head in a myriad of ways and a host of places on the earth. Chastity is essential for living in God's new pentecost when traditional morality is simply ignored and replaced by all kinds of lifestyles that exalt the creature rather than the Creator. Chastity is the way we become and remain faithful.

And then we live with obedience. Obedience is living with a responsive soul. Just as body and soul have been redefined and diminished, so too has obedience. We think of it as an action. People are "obedient" when they act in certain ways—particularly when they follow orders and do what's expected of them. And to be sure, action is part of what it means to be obedient. But before it is action, obedience is attentiveness. The word *obedience* is derived from the Latin word *oboedire*, which means to listen with the intention of putting into practice what we hear. Used in our relationship with God, *obedience* is another word for prayer.

I came to see this through the example of Jesus, who differentiated between his "work" and his "works." His works were exactly what ours are—the many things we have to do every day, the many tasks we have to perform. But his works flowed from his work—which John's Gospel tells us was the time he spent in prayer (John 5:19; 8:26). It was in such times of communion that he discovered what he was to say and what he was to do. So, Christ's obedience was an attitude before it was an action, and that is exactly what obedience means. The soul, as a "hermit within," is a soul in prayer. But such a soul will never become isolated and separated from the world. Obedience is where attentiveness and action are unified. We see and hear in order to act and speak. Living in God's new pentecost means that listening becomes living.

I believe the place where we see a spirituality of "soul" most clearly expressed is when we pray, "Thy kingdom come, thy will be done, on earth as it is in heaven." When we pray these words, we are praying as men and women who have abandoned themselves to God and are seeking to be faithful in all the ways that commitment calls for. When we pray this prayer we are being truly obedient—that is, we are listening to God with the intention to enact what we hear. And what do we hear? We hear that the coming of the Kingdom is what God wants more than anything else. As God's children, it is what we want most as well, and we offer ourselves to God as agents to bring it to pass in Jesus' Name. When we live this way, we are living "with soul."

Spirit

At first glance, the aspect of Spirit may seem to be the most obvious. We refer to the Spirit as the means by which we live a truly spiritual life. We

A New Monasticism   39

are filled with the Spirit, empowered by the Spirit, guided by the Spirit, convicted by the Spirit, gathered by the Spirit, and so on. Because this is so, we might think that we do not need to give this aspect as much attention as we have given to the body and to the soul. But I believe that is wrong. In fact, I believe that a wrong notion of the Spirit will lead to a caricature or counterfeit of Christian life. And, just as there have been aberrations with respect to the body and the soul, there have also been aberrations with respect to the Spirit. We cannot deal with all of them in a single meditation, but we can at least approach Spirit in a way that will enable us to live in a new pentecost.

We begin to establish our course when we say that Spirit is *essence*. The essence of God is Spirit, and the essence of a human is spirit. What this means from the outset is that we are not dualists. We are "of God" in the sense that we draw our life from the life of God; we always understand what it means for us to be spirit in relation to the Spirit of God. The differentiation is not between spirit and Spirit, but between humanity and deity. The differentiation is created, celebrated, and preserved in the fact that we are not God, but only made in the image of God. But the spirit/Spirit essence is what makes our relationship with God and our life for God possible.

This spirit/Spirit essence provides for our *experience*. It is Spirit that establishes the basis for the rest of the spiritual life. Were it not for the Holy Spirit, we could never dare to claim that it is possible to live as God intends. The Fall has negated the possibility of our doing that on our own. Sin has "deadened" our spirit, so that an infusion of the Holy Spirit for a new creation is as necessary as God's original "inbreathing" was in the original creation. It is in God that we live, move, and have our being (Acts 17:28). Life in a new pentecost is not an improved life, but rather a transformed life—one lived in the Spirit. Jesus provided the imagery for this in the vine-branch relationship (John 15), and for the most part we are referring to the same experience when we speak of "abiding in Christ" or being "filled with the Spirit." We are talking about a reunion of spirit/Spirit through the redemptive work of Jesus Christ. Paul later referred to it as life "in Christ" or as "Christ in you"—in either case, our hope of glory (Col 1:27).

In terms of the spiritual life, Spirit is the level of life that is beyond the senses—indeed, beyond all appearances. The things we said about the body (solitude, silence, stillness) and the soul (poverty, chastity, obedience) pave the way for an elevation into new life—what some have called "the life of God in the human soul." As we let go of all our preconceptions and attachments, we move into God's life in ways we never have before. This is what the Bible means when it speaks of seeking "the things that are above" (Col 3:1).

It is in the realm of the Sprit that we can properly speak of the spiritual life as "mystical." But we must be careful, lest we think of the mystical life as somehow abnormal, weird, or detached. I have gone out of my way in the description of body and soul to show how living in God's new pentecost *never* separates heaven and earth. The word *mystic* simply refers to a person who believes that a direct, personal relationship with God is possible and who seeks to live in ways that foster that relationship. In another sense, to be a mystic is to be a person who has exercised his or her will (through the gift of grace) in order to transcend all the elements that would otherwise have kept him or her trapped in egotism. To be a mystic is to be a person who lives in the Spirit so that Jesus may come and dwell in the heart (Eph 3:16-17).

I have known people who became so focused on "the Spirit" that they lost touch with reality and ended up with skewed perspectives. Some of them were actually scary. But I have never met a person who understood Spirit as an invitation to live in a way that is Christlike who did not provide an attractive witness to nonbelievers and also to believers. This is what happens when the spirit/Spirit union develops as it should—it makes our hearts Christ's home.

The pages of history contain story after story of people who have rejected the church, and the faith, but who still admire Jesus. Jesus is respected and revered by people of every major religion of the world. To seek to be instruments in whom he lives and through whom he works is exactly what Oswald Chambers said it was: "My utmost for His highest." For those of you who may have been waiting to see how I would connect the spiritual life and evangelism, here it is. It is living so that the Risen Christ can abide in us, and we can abide in him. Any life where that is happening is a life of witness, and that is the kind of life God asks of us in a new pentecost.

We can put all this together in the complete quotation of St. Francis. When our body, soul, and spirit are in congruence, Francis said, "The world is my cloister." By that he meant that the world becomes the place where we "walk around" as men and women created by God, redeemed by Jesus, and filled with the Spirit. We understand that abundant life is not to be hoarded but to be shared. Living in a new pentecost is putting our "whole self in"—that's what it's all about!

Disciplines for the Life

Putting our whole self before God is not something that occurs accidentally or haphazardly. It is an act of the will that engages us in the practice of the classic disciplines of the Christian spiritual life. Otherwise, we would be like a wild rosebush growing without a trellis. We would "grow in all directions" and would very quickly lose our shape and beauty. Those who work with flowers tell me that wild roses also lose their health as aberrant stems sap energy from the plant. Without "discipline" the roses will never be their best.

This is exactly what our predecessors in faith meant when they used the word *disciplines*. The disciplines were, for them, the means of grace by which the life of God is established and maintained in the human soul. Otherwise, the soul becomes a wild rose without beauty and shape—and without the health it is meant to have. Furthermore, any particular spiritual discipline is always viewed in relation to the One who is calling us to practice it. In the case of our spiritual formation it is God, whose nature is Love.

God has no interest in doing anything harmful to us, even though some of the things that are necessary are not always pleasant. When we connect the disciplines to God, we have even more reason to embrace them. They are the ordinary ways God uses to convey grace to us. No one seeking to live in a new pentecost would resist grace or shy away from anything that would increase its flow into us. So, we come to the place in this book where the conceptual and the theological merge, becoming practical and applicable. We come to the place where we pray, "God, establish in me the means through which you can pour into me abundant life."

So, we come to the disciplines. I must not assume that all who read this book have previously studied the classic spiritual disciplines. At the same time, I cannot go into detail about them.[4] I must encourage you to

---

4. If you are coming to the spiritual disciplines for the first time, I would recommend you read Richard Foster's *Celebration of Discipline* (San Francisco: HarperSanFrancisco, 1988), Susan Muto's *Pathways of Spiritual Living* (Garden City, NY: Image, 1984), and Marjorie Thompson's *Soul Feast* (Louisville: Westminster John Knox, 1995).

explore them on your own and find unique ways of practicing them. As you do this, you will become familiar with some rather standard disciplines—that is, means of grace practiced across the ages by Christians in all the traditions. You will want to concentrate upon these. But you will also find that there is no fixed list of disciplines, and you should feel the liberty to establish additional means to more fully establish you in the life God is calling you to live.

There is one essential thing that I want to get across to you in this opening meditation concerning the disciplines: they are not a grab bag of miscellaneous options. I will give you a basic list of disciplines before this chapter is over. But you must not get the idea that the spiritual disciplines are practices that are independent of each other. Nor should you think that you must make use of them all—or worse, use them all at the same time with equal devotion. This will only make you a frenetic Christian with a tendency to think that more is better. It may, in fact, make you a Christian who swallows the lie that you can "measure" your spirituality (and judge others) by the disciplines.

Instead of this, I commend to you what I learned from Dallas Willard in his excellent book *The Spirit of the Disciplines*.[5] The spiritual disciplines are the means God gives us to establish the "rhythm" of the spiritual life—the rhythm of engaging and abstaining, working and resting, doing and being. Imagine how tragic our lives would be if we could only do one thing. If all we could do is exhale, we would become depleted of life-giving oxygen. If all we could do is inhale, our lungs would eventually explode.

The spiritual life is "breathing." It is receiving and giving. It is resting and working. For some of you, this will be one of the major discoveries that you'll make by reading this book. I have met many people who have a sacred "Eureka!" moment when they realize that the Christian life has this rhythm, and that the spiritual disciplines are given to us by God to help us find that rhythm for ourselves.

So, we prayerfully select and use the disciplines that will restore this balance and rekindle the flame that this rhythm produces. If we need to practice disciplines that help us "rest," we will turn to things like sabbath, silence, and solitude. To these we may add disciplines of fasting (not just from food), frugality (simplicity), chastity, and sacrifice. If we need to practice disciplines that help us "work," we will turn to worship, study,

---

5. *The Spirit of the Disciplines* (San Francisco: HarperCollins, 1988).

prayer, service, fellowship, and submission. We will integrate the disciplines in order to develop the life.

There is no way that I can go further in a book than this. I do not know you. I don't know where you need restoration. I know that many in our day desperately need to implement the disciplines of abstinence—those disciplines that slow us down and enable us to rest in God. But I have also met people who were "stuck" in their passivity and needed to practice disciplines of engagement. The question is, where do you sense your greatest need for life? Explore the disciplines at that point and return to a practice of those things that will bring you back to your true self in Christ. From that place, you can go on to continue things you're already doing or incorporate some other new things. In the next four chapters, I will focus upon some classic disciplines that will help you do this. They are four trellis disciplines that will allow the rose that is your soul to grow and flourish in God's new pentecost.

Living by Rule

Some people equate the word *pentecostal* with "wild and crazy." But a closer look at the actual story between Acts 1:12 and 2:4 reveals another reality. From one vantage point the whole thing is noticeably orderly, even if it is unusual. The period of time covered is ten days. During each of them believers are waiting in the upper room. Some are praying; others are surely going to and from work. Meals are prepared and eaten. Sleep routines are maintained. Personal hygiene is maintained. Some community business is conducted. What ties it all together is an air of expectancy—a waiting with promise. Jesus promised something, and they believed him.

When the Spirit falls, it is not an "out of control" phenomenon that incinerates the 120 who are present. It begins with the sound of approaching wind, which when it comes fills the house like a fragrance. Tongues of fire follow, but they are "tongues" not torches; they fall but they do not destroy. No one is excluded, and there is no indication that one person got "more fire" than someone else. Even the distribution is organized and equitable.

From this vantage point, we can speak of living in God's new pentecost as living with order, not chaos. We can speak in a preliminary way about what Christians later called living with a rule of life. When God moves, it is not all over the place or all at once. There is discernible order and progress in the overall context of reality and routine. No one "goes crazy" when God comes. In fact, all the outside world can assume is that they have had a little too much to drink! But Peter puts that misconception to rest, which is another way the believers and unbelievers both had to take seriously what was happening. Unusual things—God things—are happening. But they are not things that create frenzy or spiritual "out of body" experiences.

So, when the return of Christ was delayed into the second and third centuries, the Christians tried to maintain the momentum of Pentecost by creating and maintaining an order that allowed for "signs and wonders" but not "freak shows"—a way of life that left space for surprise but not insanity, miracles but not madness. In time, this came to be called a rule of life, which was intended to establish and maintain life together. We see a classic example in the Rule of St. Benedict. But the idea of "living by rule" could also be adapted by individuals, so that their personal formation would move along in congruence with communal growth in grace.

I would not be surprised if the term *rule of life* is new to you, but I find the term is working its way back into Christian vocabulary and experience. In this chapter I will assume it is a new idea for you and approach it accordingly. I will focus on making and keeping a personal rule of life; but if you are part of a community, you may want to expand the principles to assist the group. Whether personal or corporate, a rule of life goes back to the idea of a trellis—the idea that our growth into greater Christlikeness is guided and guarded by a rule, just as the growth of a rose is promoted and protected by a trellis.

We begin with the *purpose* of a rule of life. It really only has one purpose: to help us advance in personal and social holiness, into increasing conformity to Christ. This means that when our "rule" becomes oppressive—or worse, counterproductive—we know we have misconstructed it somehow. The trellis may challenge the inclinations of the rose, but it never damages the flower. So, too, a rule of life may stretch us and lead us in directions that do not always match our personal preferences, but as we submit to the rule, we find ourselves taking on a shape that is better and more beautiful than if we had made it up as we went along. A good rule of life enables the fruit of the Spirit to grow; it enables us to live the abundant life in God's new pentecost.

The purpose of the rule leads into the *process* for making and keeping it. But before you get caught up in the mechanics of writing a rule, it's important to reflect upon the process that gives rise to a rule—namely, moving "from" something "to" something. The from/to process is at the heart of a rule and it can be about almost anything: from darkness to light, from sin to forgiveness, from illness to health, from ignorance to knowledge, from insomnia to sleep, and so on. So, the first part of the process is to ask yourself, "What do I need to move 'from' and what do I need to move 'toward'?" This means that a rule of life is an instrument to ignite a redemptive, restorative, and renewing journey.

This leads directly to the *prioritization* within a rule. If you and I make a list of formative movements, we will likely find that we could be "growing" in numerous ways. But the trellis does not allow that for a flower; nor does a rule allow that for a soul. A rule of life demands selectivity. What do I need to do most in the next three months to grow in the grace of God in Christ? That is the key question, and we do not allow our needs to overwhelm us. We trust God and allow the Spirit to work in us to choose three or four specific areas where we want to address and monitor growth.

One of the most dangerous things that we can do with a rule of life is second-guess ourselves and wonder if we picked the right things. This is no time for putting our hand to the plow and then looking back. There are all sorts of things that could be done, but we have wisely seen that we cannot do them all at once. Through a rule of life we have made some decisions. We have created some focal points. There will be time for other things later on. For now, we will give ourselves to a few things.

All this must be worked out on the *playing field* of a rule of life, which is nothing other than the days of our lives. Some of the things we have given ourselves to may need daily attention. Other things may come up on a weekly, biweekly, or monthly schedule. A few things may be monitored quarterly, semiannually, or annually. We don't have to be doing everything at once. We can spread out the growth agenda, putting it into its most natural time frames.

We come to the place of *pruning* our rule of life. Some limbs will stay on for long periods of time. Others will need to be there only until they have become a natural part of our spiritual formation. Some will only stay on for one cycle of a rule; if they need to be returned to the rule at a later time, they can be. On the other hand, in the spiritual journey, one thing leads to another. New elements will be added as fresh discoveries are made. A rule of life is dynamic, not static. It allows for change as our need for change arises. Each edition of our rule of life is an expression of current reality that will evolve into future development.

As we bring this chapter to a close, let's go back to the biblical text. When the original manifestations of the first Pentecost had settled down, the Christians found themselves with three thousand new believers at the end of the first day! The need for a rule of life was essential and immediate. Luke describes that rule in 2:42–47. It included these elements: apostolic teaching, fellowship, prayers, life together, sharing of possessions, worship, and eating together in homes. They didn't call it a rule of life, but it was their way of working out the salvation they had experienced. And that's what a rule of life is.

Worship

Worship is the central act of the people of God. It is the context within which a rule of life is shaped and our life with God is sustained. Before the first generation of Christians had died, worship on "the Lord's day" was an established part of their spiritual formation. The reason for this is simple; as N. T. Wright puts it, "When we begin to glimpse the reality of God, the natural reaction is to worship him."[6] We must give that which is ultimate in us to that which is Ultimate in the universe. We do that by worship. When the Spirit falls on us, our spirits rise to God.

All of life can be an act of worship. But as with anything else in life, we "punctuate" our generic experiences with specific moments. We live all the time, but once a year we celebrate our birthday. If we are married, we are married twenty-four hours a day, but we mark our wedding anniversary with a special event or ceremony. We believe in hygiene, but we choose when to bathe and brush our teeth. We acknowledge the need for sleep, but then we actually go to bed in order to get some. Every part of life is a combination of the ongoing and the specific.

Worship is surely a continuous act, but we must also reserve moments and occasions for it. Otherwise, it will be difficult to sustain the larger, continuous reality. If I tell you that I have a friend and that we are "very close," you might ask me, "So, how often do you all get together?" If

---

6. N. T. Wright, *Simply Christian* (San Francisco: HarperSanFrancisco, 2006) 143.

I responded by saying, "I haven't seen him in years," you would question how "close" we actually are. And you would have every right to do so.

The same holds true of our relationship with God. We cannot claim intimacy and friendship with God when it's been "years" since we've been with Him. Imagine a chef saying, "I work with food all day long, so I don't need to stop and eat." In about two weeks we would be reading his obituary in the newspaper. The generic cannot be sustained apart from the specific. Acts of worship must punctuate our ongoing life of worship. As William Temple put it, there must be set times when we "worship, pure and simple."

But how we worship is another question. Over the years I have watched people opt in and out of worship, depending on its style. They attended worship they "liked" and absented themselves from worship they "disliked." Even writing these words on paper should show how mistaken this notion is. It puts the focus on the activities of worship rather than the God of worship. Of course, we have our preferences in worship, just as we have preferences for everything else. But we do not worship our preferences; we worship God!

But even while we acknowledge the legitimate variety of worship styles, we must call ourselves to rise above them to see what the elements are in any valid worship. How do we worship God in a new pentecost? Jesus gave few specific instructions about how we worship, but on one occasion he did say we are to worship God "in spirit and in truth" (John 4:24). We can use this statement to frame a general theology of worship.

We worship God *in spirit*. Whatever else this may mean, it means that we worship God from the deepest part of who we are—human beings who have decided to follow Jesus. Both dimensions are important. We worship as human beings made in the image of God. And we worship as human beings who have oriented our entire lives in relation to Christ. Every act of worship is the presentation of our selves to God as living sacrifices (Rom 12:1). That's what worship "in spirit" implies. We open our lives as completely as we can to relate to God as comprehensively as we can.

We also worship God *in truth*. The word *truth* continues the idea of our in-depth authenticity. But it also means we worship in ways that reflect our desire to be "told" the truth so that we can "live" the truth. We do not worship just to feel good; we worship to feel godly. And sometimes, the only way that can happen is if we allow the Holy Spirit to cut us to the heart (e.g., Acts 2:37). We have mistakenly called this "hellfire and damnation preaching," but to view worship this way is to completely miss the point. The Pentecost story shows that the crowd was never more on the verge of coming to life than when they were cut to the heart. It wasn't "hellfire and damnation," it was "heavenly light and life." But it came in a form that had to convict before it could convert.

We want to know the truth of worship, but we do so in order that we might live the truth, not merely understand it. Whether the truth encounter comes in our daily devotional time or in a formal service of worship in a church, we bow down so that we can rise up. We enter the presence of God in the sanctuary so that we can bear witness to the ways of God in the world. The test of worship's authenticity is not how "well" it was conducted, or "the blessing" we received from it. The test of worship is whether we come to the end of it with greater desire and ability (through the Spirit) to fulfill the two great commandments (Matt 22:37–40). We evaluate the quality of our worship by the increase of love in our lives.

Worship in God's new pentecost is essential. Simply put, we cannot claim to work for God without walking with Him. We are not employees who carry out God's commands; rather, we are beloved sons and daughters who dwell in the Father's presence (e.g., John 15:15). Too many of us have settled for an "outside in the yard" relationship with God, when God wants us to have an "inside the house" relationship. Worship is God's invitation to come inside where the Spirit/spirit experience occurs and where the Friend/friend relationship is cultivated. Worship is the occasion when we catch our best glimpse of who God is, so that we can receive God's picture of who we are.

It is no accident that when the monastic movement shifted from being hermetical (monks living in isolation) to being cenobitic (monks living in community), worship shaped the common life of the monks. Saint Benedict called worship "the work of God"—the supreme activity to which we are called and in which we are involved. From that heritage we continue to receive, reflect, and respond to God. Worship is at the heart of life in God's new pentecost.

Prayer

Go into any monastery or convent, and the first thing that will strike you is how quiet the place is. The slightest sound echoes through the hallways and bounces around the rooms. This is because the monastic life is the life of prayer. Life in a new pentecost is also a life centered in continuous prayer—what the Apostle Paul referred to as praying without ceasing (1 Thess 5:17). In every branch of Christianity, prayer is the chief means of grace. This is because it is our primary speech. And when prayer is truly practiced, God gets the first word—the "wordless" word, the word spoken without sound. God speaks; everything else is response.[7]

To say that life in a new pentecost is prayerful is to say that it is contemplative. I cannot do justice to the rich word *contemplation* in a brief meditation, but I must point to it if you are to understand the importance of prayer when the wind of the Spirit is blowing. To say that prayer is contemplative is to say that God is the "template," and our primary task is to be "with" God: *con templatio*, "with the template."

At this point, we are not describing any particular form of prayer. We are referring to the disposition of prayer. We are saying what the Bible says in several places—that our first and primary act is to "incline our hearts unto the Lord." Wherever there is an incline, it means that the person above can roll a ball down to the person below. With respect to prayer, it means God can send any "word" to us and it will roll in our direction, because our hearts are "inclined" to God. The silence of monasteries and convents is an indication that an environment of "inclination" has been established for the benefit of each individual and the community as a whole.

It would be incorrect to look at the pre-Pentecostal period of ten days and overlay it with any historic expression of monasticism. But I do believe it is fair to say that the Christians described in the upper room were inclining their hearts to the Lord. They were disposed to attentiveness. They were listening for the next word God would speak to them. They were readying themselves for the next revelation. They were living in a receptive mode. This is where prayer begins, and this is why it is the central discipline in the Christian life.

Although I have no desire to be unkind to anyone, I have to raise the question, do we live in an environment of inclination? When we enter many churches today, instead of silence we find noise. Conversations begun in the parking lot continue in the sanctuary. There is no break from speaking to listening, from sound to silence. We are invited to stand and to say or sing something. What one person has called "noisy worship"

---

7 Eugene Peterson has influenced my understanding of prayer as "primary speech" in his book *Tell It Slant* (Grand Rapids: Eerdmans, 2008).

continues in some churches for forty to forty-five minutes. Between each song a worship leader "keeps talking" in a way that is more about segues than sacredness.

What little time there is for silence feels more like "dead air" than an opportunity to pray. And we don't want too much of it, lest people become fidgety or uncomfortable. Overstimulated people cannot handle a lot of silence. So, it's not long before we are speaking or singing again. And when the final song is sung, the congregation instantly resumes the chatter that was going on an hour or so ago. Do we live in an environment of inclination? Do we allow God to have the first word? Do we pray?

These questions are not meant as indictments, but they are intended to raise serious issues. For if we cease to pray, we cease to live. A true pentecostal experience deteriorates into a religious "production" where we have a form of godliness but deny the power thereof. We say some prayers but we do not pray. We do not give God the opportunity to speak the first word. We are not an "inclined" people. We are more likely to try to manufacture a revelation than to receive one. Without realizing it, we lose the "vertical" in favor of the "horizontal." And in time, we forget there ever was a "vertical" to begin with—perhaps even criticizing or caricaturing those who try to preserve it.

If there is a fresh wind blowing, if there is a return to a God priority, what kind of prayer will express this renewal—and also maintain it? I have come to believe that it will be through a revival of liturgical prayer. (Some of you may have to lay the book down and walk around for a little while after reading that last sentence.) But I hope you won't give up on me, and I hope you won't second-guess what I mean by the phrase "liturgical prayer." I hope you will keep reading so that you can see whether you agree that life in a new pentecost is rooted in liturgical prayer.

By liturgical prayer, I essentially mean prayer that is given to us by the church. I am not sure that everyone defines it this way, but that is what I mean by it—at least what I mean by it in this meditation. To say that prayer is "given" is another way of saying that it is speech that comes to us; we do not make it up as we go along. Without overstating the case, I would like to propose that liturgical prayer is how God comes to us, and how we in turn respond.

Where do we find the best theology of the faith? We find it in the liturgy of the church. Why? Because it is in the liturgy where the church achieves consensus about what matters most, and it is in the liturgy where the church invites us to profess our faith. When we pray liturgically, we pray the faith. And if we have been properly catechized, we also pray *our* faith. The church gives us the words, and we gladly and heartily pray them back to God. We do this because the words glorify God, edify us, and shape us into the disciples Christ calls us to be. We do not "read" the prayers, we *pray* them, because they resonate with the deepest convictions of our hearts and the most concrete expressions of our lives.

When the church prays liturgically, it does not simply pray what's on the page. The best liturgy includes "spaces" for silence where individual and collective petitions can be included. I have sat in worship services where people really knew how to do this well, and the interweaving of written and unwritten prayers was so natural that I could hardly tell where one stopped and the other began. When I speak of "liturgical prayer," I am not speaking of prayers printed in a book, but rather prayers imprinted upon our souls. Some of them will be written, and others will be extemporaneous. Some will be formal, and others will be informal. Some will be spoken, and others will be silent.

Liturgical prayer is living prayer. It takes its life from the life of the church and the faith it professes. It gives its life from the individual hearts and collective spirit that make the church the Body of Christ. Liturgical prayer is "inhaling" the revelation and "exhaling" the response. It is allowing God to have the first word, and following with all the secondary words that are necessary to give praise to God and to receive guidance from God.

Liturgical prayer is pentecostal prayer, also, because it invites a person to enter into a life of prayer that already exists. The newcomer is not left to wonder how to pray, or to impose his or her way of praying on the rest. Liturgical prayer exists in the spirit of the Lord's Prayer—in the spirit of Jesus, who responded to the request of the disciples to teach them to pray by giving them an actual prayer. They were not limited to the sixty-plus words that were spoken, even though I'm sure they often prayed it together, as we do today. But they were given a pattern, a template, which they could be "with" as they prayed individually and collectively.

As I have said at other points in this book, I want all this to be invitational. So, here and now, I want to invite you into the silence. I want to invite you into the place where God can speak the first word, and where you can respond. I want to invite you to make use of some kind of liturgy, so that prayer can be a "gift" to you from the church, not just words you try to come up with on your own on the spur of the moment. I want to invite you to *pray* the liturgy, not just recite it. I want to invite you to mingle your own petitions with those given to you, so that prayer as "breathing" (inhaling and exhaling) can occur. I want to invite you into the life of prayer, where heart-to-heart communion can happen. This is prayer in God's new pentecost.

Lectio Divina

In the last meditation I called prayer "primary speech." I did not invent the phrase, but I like it. As I said, it puts the beginning of prayer in the right place—in God. God prays first (revelation), and then we pray (response). Therefore, prayer for us is first of all listening. This is why the church says over and over, "*Hear* the word of God." We have already spoken of how the church does this in worship. We must now meditate on the means by which we do it individually and in groups.

The historic name for it is *lectio divina*—divine reading. It is actually a form of prayer, because it is the means for allowing God to speak first. But it is also a method for receiving and responding to what we hear. It is a method that can incorporate all other Bible study methods. But it is a method in its own right that any Christian can practice authentically and meaningfully. I believe it is the method for a new pentecost, because it does not compete with other methods, but rather invites all believers into an ongoing dialogue of prayer with Scripture and other texts in varying levels of expertise and desire.

We include it in a book on living in God's new pentecost because all Christian traditions make searching the Scriptures the second most important discipline. In fact, because lectio divina is a form of prayer, we may prefer not to think of it as a second discipline at all, but rather as an extension of the first. In liturgical prayer we are praying the life of faith and our lives as Christians. In lectio divina we are praying the Word. They are threads in a seamless tapestry of spirituality, where the Divine Word and the human word become congruent means of grace.

Lectio divina has an identifiable process, but it is a mistake to think of the elements as "steps." They are more like swirling dynamics that interact to enable the written Word to become the living Word in us. We do not practice one of them and then leave it behind for the next one. Instead, we "incline our heart to the Lord" and let the elements dispose us to read, mark, and inwardly digest the message. Our spirituality becomes increasingly "Word-shaped," because Jesus is the living Word who is made known to us in the written Word.

Lectio begins with reading. That's literally what the word *lectio* means. But it is not just any kind of reading. It is reading a text in the form and order in which it is written. Lectio assumes that greater wisdom can be gained from reading a text as it has been given to us, not in bits and pieces. When it comes to the Bible, we believe that revelation is, in part, connected to its organization. While we can move here and there when we read the Bible, and while some devotional guides take a nonsequential approach, lectio divina proceeds by starting at the beginning and moving toward the end of a particular book of the Bible.[8]

In the phase of lectio, we read until a word or phrase strikes us. When that happens, we stop. We do not second-guess why this happened. Lectio is a phase where we read receptively. We do not waste time or energy asking why we were drawn to a particular portion of the reading. We may discover later in the process why something happened. But in the phase of reading, we honor the impression by pausing to reflect upon the word or phrase that has attracted our attention. This piece of the text becomes the basis for the rest of the lectio divina process.

In classic lectio divina this is called "taking a word." The idea is analogous to picking fruit. God has provided the fruit, and we have been drawn to one particular piece of it. We pick it—and we do not question why we chose one piece of fruit instead of another. We simply take it and prepare to eat it, in order that we may receive the nourishment that it is created to give. In the same way, we may think of the whole passage as the fruit tree and the particular word or phrase as the piece of fruit that we reach out and pluck.

With that "word" in hand, we move into meditation. We take the fruit and go beneath its peel. We take the word and penetrate its surface. The word *meditate* is interesting in its own right. It conjures the image of a cow chewing its cud. The cow eats and swallows. Then it brings the food back up for additional chewing. The cow repeats this process until it has gotten "the maximum" nourishment out of the food. Meditation on a

---

8. This does not mean that a random reading is invalid, nor does it mean that we cannot do lectio unless we read sequentially. We are speaking about the way in which lectio divina yields its best fruit, which is as it follows the "revelational flow" of a text.

text is similarly repetitive; we revisit it, looking at it from multiple vantage points, so that we can get the most out of it.

Here is the phase when we can bring our best skills to lectio divina. Some people can do formal exegesis. Others can work in the original biblical languages. Still others can make use of study tools like commentaries and concordances. We can also read the text through the lens of multiple characters (if the text is a story) or through a range of emotions that the text evokes. We are piercing; we are pondering; we are getting all the nourishment that we can out of the portion of text that we have taken.

Most likely, the meditation phase will give rise to multiple discoveries. We select one or two and limit the rest of our meditation to them. In the same way that we do not try to "take in" the whole passage, we do not try to ponder all the ideas that have come to us during the meditative process. We may or may not choose to write them all down, and it may be that the Holy Spirit will bring one of the unchosen ideas back to us for further attention. But the meditative phase draws to a close with a simple selection of one or two ideas. We might ask this question: Which of the ideas is most important for me to consider right now? We do not second-guess our decision; we focus on the choice we have made and "chew on it" a little more.

Meditation flows right into contemplation. The "template" is the idea or two we have taken from the text portion. In contemplation, we seek to be "with" (*con*) the template (the idea). We pray, "God let me be what your Word is." For example, if the text portion is about patience, we pray to become patient. If it calls for honesty, we pray to become more honest. Contemplation is the phase of lectio divina where the written Word becomes the living Word. The idea on paper ignites in our souls. Contemplation may very well add to our knowledge, but more than acquisition, it brings us to encounter. Some people refer to contemplation as "resting in the Word," but this is not a passive moment; it is a receptive moment—a moment to stop working on the text and let the text work on us.

Classic lectio divina ends in contemplation. However, many contemporary models add a final step of "action"—just so there is no doubt about the ultimate purpose of lectio divina. Our predecessors knew that there is no true contemplation that does not result in living faith. But in our day, when too many people read the Bible without actually living it, it is important to emphasize that action is the intended outcome. We alluded to it above, but we repeat it here. Again, if we find that the text is about patience, we end lectio divina by praying for the grace to become even more patient in our life with Christ. If we desire to "be" what the Word "is" in contemplation, then in action we desire to "do" what the Word "is" in actual behavior.

These phases can be done each day as we engage in our private times of devotion. We can also make use of them in small groups where we bring our insights to the community for sharing, further interpretation, and enactment. Groups can agree to read assigned passages between group meetings and bring their findings back to the next session. Sometimes, they may also choose to actually read a passage together during the group meeting and go through the lectio phases at the same time.

Lectio divina is the kind of reading we are called to do as we live in God's new pentecost. It is reading that is actually prayer—reading that becomes a sacred conversation between the Holy Spirit and our human spirit. It is reading that has a formative effect upon us, conforming us to the image of Christ. And it is reading that brings life to the church and the world in Jesus' name. It is reading that enables us to actually experience what we pray: "thy kingdom come, thy will be done, on earth as it is in heaven."

Dynamics in the New Monasticism

Our look at the disposition, dimensions, and disciplines of the new monasticism has taken us into the details of it. We have gone beneath the surface and opened a conversation regarding key elements that are required of us if we are to live in God's new pentecost. There is more that we could explore, and I have provided direction as to what you might do when you've finished this book. But we have come to the place where we need to step back from the trees and regain a vision of the forest. We need to look at the overarching dynamics that occur as we seek to be faithful.

There are many ways to describe these dynamics, but one classic phrase is "the conversion of life." By choosing this phrase I am intending to make it clear that life in a new pentecost is not about tinkering; it is about transformation. We do not say, "We want to be better persons." We say, "We want to be different persons." That's what the word *conversion* implies, and it is what life in a new pentecost requires. We are not even out to become more committed; we are on a journey to become Christlike.

We do not minimize this. We do not hide this. And most of all, we do not pull a religious version of "bait and switch" after people become associated with us. Right at the start we say, "We are out to convert ourselves, and you, to Jesus."

My friend Will Willimon sparked this in me when I heard him say that we have no need to apologize for being this clear and this bold. The drug dealer on the street and the advertising expert on television are not apologetic. They have one aim—conversion. They want to get people on their side. Will says that if the world is so bold, why should Christians be any less so? I agree. Moreover, I find this spirit characterized the believers who came down from the upper room and bore witness to their experience to the Pentecost crowds in Jerusalem. When some in that crowd asked what they were to do in response, Peter did not tiptoe around the question or soft-pedal the requirements. He said, "Repent, and be baptized every one of you in the name of Jesus Christ for the forgiveness of your sins, and you shall receive the gift of the Holy Spirit" (Acts 2:38). This is conversion of life. It was the intent of the first Pentecost; it is the intent of any new pentecost until Jesus comes again.[9]

But we need more than a one-word description. *Conversion* is the right word, but it is not an all-sufficient word. *Conversion* is the right word, but it is a word that has been variously used over time in Christian communities. If it is to make sense in this book, you must know what I mean by it and how I am offering it to you. Several ideas are contained within it—ideas that bring about the transformation we see as essential for living in a new pentecost.

First, we understand the word in its literal sense: "to turn." The conversion of life is a process, not a moment. There may surely be an initiating moment (called "new birth" by some), but it will not be the only moment. All you have at a birth is a baby. Conversion is a "turning." I believe Jesus was speaking about it this way when he issued his first call to the disciples: "Come after me, and I will make you to become fishers of men" (Mark 1:17, literal Greek). Jesus' use of the words *make* and *become* indicates that he understood conversion to be a process. It does not occur all at once. Babies are made to grow up.

Second, to turn is to experience two things simultaneously. We are "turning from" something and "turning toward" something. This image is

---

9. I believe Jonathan Wilson-Hartgrove has it right when he uses the phrase "School(s) for Conversion" to describe the new monasticism.

what has given rise to the Christian life as a journey in classical spiritual formation. We are "leaving behind" and "moving ahead" when we are experiencing the conversion of life. This settles once and for all whether the Christian life is more about the confession of sin or growth in sanctification. It is both. Think of it this way: when I move away from a wall that I have been leaning against and begin to move toward another wall that has captured my attention, I am "leaving" and "moving toward" all at once.

The spiritual life is a never-ending "from-to" experience. At one moment, I may be dealing with sin, but as I do so, I make progress. At another moment, I may be making progress, but as I do so, I am becoming more victorious over sin. We need to see the conversion of life as "breathing." We do not dissect breathing into inhaling and exhaling, and then value one over the other. We breathe, and as we do, inhaling and exhaling occur as they were intended to.

Finally, the conversion of life is the conversion of *life*. The final evidence that our spiritual life is authentic is that we actually live differently. We cannot do this apart from a change of heart and a change of mind. But the proof is in a change of will. We simply do not do what we used to do. Or, to view it from the other angle, we do what God has willed for us to do from the moment we were conceived. We live as Christ.

This is why we cannot water down the Gospel or life in God's new pentecost. We are not writing the Story, we are telling it. We are not the creators of the Message, we are stewards of it. If we alter or diminish it, we dishonor Christ and we offer people waxed fruit rather than the real thing. We simply cannot do this. We are not called to arrange things so that we will always be pleasing to the world. We are called to proclaim things so that we will always be pleasing to Jesus. Our message is the conversion of life.

The Mystical Way

In the history of Christian spirituality, the conversion of life is not a vague or indescribable experience. Just as we develop our disposition, dimensions, and disciplines within a rule of life, we develop our conversion of life within an identifiable framework. There are a variety of ways to talk about this. But in a language that is part of the new monasticism, the conversion of life is following "the mystical way." I will use this way of looking at it to further describe the dynamics of living in God's new pentecost.

For some, we must deal with the word *mystical*. Along the way, it has taken on a negative connotation. Some of the negativism is due to misunderstanding, but some of it is due to the bad witness of some who have claimed to be "mystics." I remember teaching about this years ago, and before I had barely begun, someone in the room spoke up, "Well, I'll tell you one thing, I don't want to be a mystic!" Several others nodded their heads in agreement, and I had to dig myself out of a hole that the word had opened. I'm not sure I ever regained unanimous support, but I will share with you what I said that brought most of the detractors back into the fold.

The word *mystic* simply means someone who believes that a direct experience with God is possible. It is a person who understands that experience is part of the Christian life, along with such things as Scripture, tradition, and reason. If you can sing, "You ask me how I know he lives; he lives within my heart," you are a mystic. Don't let the fact that the word has been used in inaccurate and misleading ways cause you to give it up. In the history of Christisn spirituality, *mysticism* is a rich word. It is a word that affirms the fact that we are made in the image of God, and therefore we have a capacity for relationship with God, and God with us. If you can sing, "He walks with me and talks with me, and tells me I am his own," you are a mystic.

Furthermore, the word *mystic* means a person who is connected to the great cloud of witnesses and to the faith once delivered to the saints. Only counterfeit mystics are freelance. True mystics are consciously and conscientiously part of the Christian tradition and the church. Mystics are not Lone Rangers. To borrow Robert Fulghum's words, they "hold hands and stick together." In short, mystics are any and all of us who believe that we can live in Christ and that Christ can live in us. With this corrected view, we can move on to look at the stages of faith that are part of the mystical way.

It begins with *purgation*. The Christian journey launches with our recognition that we need to repent before we can be renewed; we need to become empty before we can be filled. Because we are sinful, we must be purged of some things before we can be empowered or purified by other things. The essential purgation is to be cleansed and freed from egotism—what Thomas Merton and others have called "the false self." We are no longer selves turned in on ourselves or selves relying upon ourselves.

From that foundational purgation, we are now abandoned to God in ways that allow all sorts of other purgations to occur when and where they are needed. To read the biographies of the saints or to listen to the testimony of other Christians is to discover the many ways God comes into our lives to "clean house" so that we can become temples of the Holy Spirit.

From this purgation, we enter into *illumination*. Think of it like contacts or a pair of glasses. A dirty lens keeps the light from coming in, and it also skews the way things on the outside look to us. We clean our contacts and our glasses so that we can see things as they are. Illumination is our ability to see ourselves and the world as God intends. Purgation cleans the lenses. Illumination follows. As the word implies, it is an experience of enlightenment—"the people who walked in darkness have seen a great light" (Isa 9:2). And when we have sufficient light, we can walk into the future with confidence and discernment.

It is important to emphasize that our illumination is focused on our ability to see Jesus. We see it occurring in the disciples, who after the illumination of the resurrection could see the Risen Christ. We see it in the apostolic community, which found its life in a bright vision of Jesus as Lord. We see it in the classic Christianity described by Thomas á Kempis in his *Imitation of Christ*, where a transforming vision of Christ leads to a corresponding life *in* Christ and *for* Christ. We are illuminated by his Light.

The next step in the mystical way is "the dark night of the soul." It is almost dangerous to try to write about this in a single meditation. But we cannot properly look at the mystical way without noting it. The dark night of the soul is not the same thing as spiritual dryness, although there is some overlap in the two concepts. The dark night of the soul is God's act in our lives to see if our love for Him is based upon the benefits we gain from it, or whether it is love for God alone.[10]

This is not a comfortable phase in the journey, but it is a necessary one. If we have faith only because it is good, we have yet to discover a faith that exists because *God* is good. If we believe only because of the blessings, we will either struggle to believe or cease to believe when the blessings fade away—as they do, sooner or later. No experience can be sustained indefinitely. There is an ebb and flow in all of life. There is an ebb and flow in the spiritual life too. So, God must work in us to insure that we do not

---

10. The classic work on this is Bernard of Clairvaux's *The Four Loves*.

"rise and fall" as life rises and falls. We must not stop with being Christian because we get a lot out of it. We must be led to the place where we are Christian even when our senses are not providing any confirmations or consolations.

I believe we see Jesus' dark night of the soul in the Garden of Gethsemane. All the supports were falling away. His three best friends were sleeping. Satan was coming back to try one last time to get him to give up the mission. It was literally night, but it was also night in his soul, as Jesus begged that the cup might pass from him. And then we read these words: "Nevertheless, not my will but yours be done" (Matt 26:39). The word *nevertheless* is the word that shows us that Jesus had moved from a sensory faith to a God-alone faith. It is our word when we face enormous challenges, grievous injustices, and painful experience—*nevertheless* we believe.

When we do this, we come to that place in the mystical way called *union*. We do not become God, but we become "one with" God—a state in which we intend only what God intends, where we want only what God wants, where we promote only what God desires. In historic Christian vocabulary, this is called "Christian perfection." It has also been called "singleness of intention." It is not teetotal flawlessness, but it is a complete identification with God and God's will—a union of wills, a oneness between Spirit and spirit. Yet, even this is not a stage of arrival as much as it is a phase of intentionality. We are dealing with the infinite God, so we never come to the "end" of the Christian experience. But we can be one with God every day of our lives, in that we come to the place where we get up every morning wanting to live our lives for Christ. This is what the Bible means when it refers to the Spirit-filled life. This is the goal for every Christian.

Marks of a New Monasticism

Before we bring our exploration of a new monasticism to a close, we must ask and respond to the question, what is all this for? We have spoken in some detail about the disposition of our hearts and the development of our lives through intentional practices that are both private and communal. We have used intensive words like *transformation* and *the conversion of life* to make it clear that we are not commending a mere tinkering with life, a few small adjustments that we can label "new and improved." Rather,

A New Monasticism 61

raising our sails so that the wind of the Spirit can fill them and direct us is an act that is intended to produce a new kind of person and a new kind of community.

As I have studied the new monasticism and entered into the fringes of it myself, I have become aware of a dozen "marks" that were adopted by twenty communities in 2004 and have been shared by others since then.[11] They are the core values and holy habits that the new monasticism seeks to instill in those who become part of it. With respect to this book, we may think of everything in relation to the two great commandments. What I have said up to now can be thought of as relating to the command to love God.

The dozen marks of a new monasticism can be viewed as relating to the command to love our neighbor as ourselves. In actuality, the two dynamics are part of a whole, but it is necessary for us to see them distinctively in order to fully grasp what God is doing on the earth today. So, I want to conclude this section with a brief commentary on each of the dozen characteristics. As I do so, it will be clear that the kind of life I've previously described—most especially a life lived by grace and in Christ— is necessary if we are to adopt these marks as evidence that we are actually participating in the new pentecost.

The first mark of a new monasticism is *locating our lives in the abandoned places of the empire*. God never leaves any space, but we sometimes do. We leave places of suffering for places of comfort. We relocate to the suburbs and leave the inner city to collapse further upon itself. In doing so, we create the illusion that we are doing well, when in fact we are only reproducing Christianity in ways that suit us. But worst of all, we forget that Christ has remained in the places of suffering—in deteriorating inner cities and in other places where the will of God is not being done on earth. A new monasticism opens our eyes to not only what we have done, but also what we now need to do. A new monasticism is fundamentally a recovery movement.

Second, a new monasticism practices *shared economics*. North American capitalism is based on private ownership and individual possessions. Gospel economics is based on the spirit of stewardship. We do not place a certain percentage of our money and possessions before God, but

---

11. These marks have been published for the good of an even wider fellowship of Christians: *School(s) for Conversion: 12 Marks of a New Monasticism* (Eugene, OR: Cascade Books, 2005).

rather we live with an attitude that says, "All that I have is from You and for You. Show me what and how you want me to share what I have with others." Because we do this before a loving God, we need not fear scarcity, for God will seek our welfare as much as the welfare of another. But we will find that stewardship loosens our grip on things and tightens our grip on the hand of God.

A third characteristic of a new monasticism is *hospitality*. While this quality may be expressed in many different ways, it essentially means opening our hearts and our homes to others. Often this will include friends whom we know, but it will also mean people we do not know. Sometimes this will mean a literal provision of space, but at other times it will mean creating the space of attentiveness so that we can really listen to what others are trying to tell us through their words and actions. Hospitality begins in attentiveness and becomes incarnate through a will devoted to doing the will of God once it is known.

Fourth, a new monasticism fosters *reconciliation*. Through Christ, God has reconciled us to Himself, and has given us the ministry of reconciliation (2 Cor 5:18). The need for racial reconciliation remains, and we must remain steadfast in our efforts to increase it. But a new monasticism gives us "eyes to see" the need for reconciliation in many others areas of life—between husbands and wives, parents and children, employers and employees; between rich and poor, privileged and dispossessed, governments and their citizens. We may find the need for reconciliation right in our own families, schools, offices, and churches. Allowing the Spirit to blow "fresh wind" into our lives means that we will seek reconciliation wherever we see a need for it.

Fifth, a new monasticism encourages *submission to Christ's Body, the church*. This is not exclusively a passive acceptance of everything said and done in and by the church. It includes playing the role of loving critic when we see the visible church failing to incarnate the invisible Church. Consequently, our submission is not ultimately to the institution (that's where the word *loyalty* comes in), but rather to the Body. A new monasticism will be ecumenical in spirit and eclectic in makeup, but it will not become a "substitute church" to use as an excuse for not being faithful members of our respective ecclesial organizations. Within our specific loyalties, we will honor the church's profession of faith and its leaders, and we will work under its supervision to manifest the Kingdom of God upon the earth.

New monastics will always be *active members* of their community, while claiming their higher identity as *disciples of Jesus*.

Sixth, a new monasticism promotes *formation in the way of Christ*. We understand this essentially to be growth in the fruit of the Spirit, as applied to the fulfillment of the two great commandments. Consequently, we come against any expressions of faith that are judgmental, arrogant, or legalistic. Instead, we seek to be agents of God's love (*agape*) in whatever ways we can. In order to do this, we understand that we must practice the spiritual disciplines, which shape us inwardly, outwardly, and corporately. There is no discipleship without discipline, and there is no discipline without the practice of the disciplines.

Seventh, a new monasticism is intent upon *nurturing a common life*. Humility is the hallmark of this spirit of nurture. We do not think in terms of independence, but rather interdependence. We do not create hierarchies, but rather consider ourselves servants of one another. This commitment is rooted deeply in Christ's own apostolic fellowship and in the early Christian communities. In fact, there is no form of community that can properly be called "Christian" where life together is not the defining element.

Eighth, a new monasticism *celebrates singleness and marriage*. Jesus celebrated singleness when he commended those who had made themselves eunuchs for the sake of the Kingdom, and when he lived as a single man himself. He celebrated marriage by blessing the wedding at Cana of Galilee and speaking of the holy union that marriage creates between a man and a woman. The celebration in both states is not sex, but love—love that cares, protects, supports, encourages, nurtures, forgives, and sustains. A new monasticism becomes what the early monastics called "a school of love" and provides room (literally and figuratively) for love to grow.

Ninth, a new monasticism encourages *geographic proximity*. This may include actually living together in one house. But it means more than that. It means determining whether there are other communities nearby that seek the same kind of faithfulness in God's new pentecost. It means establishing partnerships and engaging in mutually beneficial ministries. Overall, it means "lowering the walls" on our respective groups and institutions and joining hands with people around us to be formed into greater maturity and sent into greater mission.

A tenth characteristic of a new monasticism is *care for creation*. As with other marks previously discussed, this includes but is not limited to a single issue, such as care for the environment. It includes being a better steward of the earth's diminishing resources. It means looking at local issues of public health and safety and advocating principles and practices that promote health and welfare. It means making little changes where we can (e.g., driving less and walking more). It means volunteering where we can to make actual improvements. It means working with social workers and civic planners, who know far better than we do how pollution and degradation harm people.

Eleventh, a new monasticism practices *peacemaking*. Most of the time, this means beginning with interrupting some kind of conflict. It means upsetting someone's apple cart. But that is only the beginning. Peacemaking's goal is to replace conflict with construction. It is moving from injustice to justice, from estrangement to restoration, and from hostility to forgiveness. It also means "seeing the invisible"—that is, challenging people to expand their vision, to move from things as they are to things as they could be. We sometimes view peacemaking in terms of the first five letters ("peace") and forget that it actually means the last six ("making").

Finally, a new monasticism centers itself in *contemplative prayer*. This is simply recognizing that we are to abide in Christ and that apart from him we can do nothing (John 15:4). It is acknowledging that supernatural tasks require supernatural power, and that any and all of our actions must flow from and be guided by the Risen Christ. Being rooted in contemplative prayer means that we are not trying to get God to do what we want, but rather trying to dwell so close to God's heart that we discern what He wants. A new monasticism views a surrendered life as the most beautiful and powerful experience we can have.

At the beginning of this book we used the analogy of raising our sails so that the Holy Spirit can fill them and direct us. The preceding marks are enough to inspire us in the offering of our lives to God—as Paul put it—as "living sacrifices" (Rom 12:1). Once we realize that we have the opportunity to live this way, it becomes an invitation that carries with it the very "fire of God"—a fire that burns in and through us like nothing else can do.

THREE
A New Order

LIVING IN ORDER

The final section of this book is intentionally practical. When an invitation is extended and it anticipates an RSVP, the recipients need to know when and how to respond. I believe this is the case in responding to God's invitation to become part of a new pentecost. So, the remaining meditations are down-to-earth instructions for turning our "yes" to God into individual and communal realities. I have chosen to use the idea of forming a spiritual order to speak about the specific responses we can make.

Like the term *new monasticism*, the term *spiritual order* is not to be viewed exclusively in the historic sense. There are transferrable concepts for us to make use of, and there may be some limited cases where you will want to literally form some kind of order to give expression to your commitments. But more likely, you will use the idea of an "order" metaphorically. I trust your creativity and your following of the Spirit when it comes to these things. But I do believe some connection with Christian history can be helpful as we begin this last section of the book.

The history of Christianity shows that in times when a fresh wind of the Spirit is blowing, Christians strengthen their life together in community. It is no passing matter that on the first Pentecost the believers were "all together in one place." It is no small thing that in times of renewal, God's Spirit draws us close to one another. As we move toward the end of our meditations on a new pentecost, we must give attention to the call to live in unity and formative fellowship.

Throughout these meditations I have intentionally woven the thread of life together into the tapestry of this book's message. And I have written about my conviction that God is calling Christians to be domestic monks—that is, men and women who continue to live in the world, but who do so with a sense of communally directed life and purpose. My choice of the word *monk* is intentional, because it speaks on the one hand of our singular devotion to Christ, and on the other hand of our commitment to community. Monks are lovers of Jesus who live in monasteries. In a new pentecost disciples are lovers of Jesus who live in community. This is what I mean by the phrase "living in order." Christ is our Center, and we then find ourselves on the circumference of interpersonal and ecclesial relationships.

I believe it is possible that a few of you who read this book may want to explore a formal monastic life. This is easy to do. If you think God may be calling you to a formal monastic life, I would counsel you to look at the main expressions of it before you make a final decision. You can go online to learn more about the Benedictines, the Cistercians, the Carmelites, the Carthusians, the Franciscans, and other historic orders. There are orders in Protestantism and Orthodoxy as well. In addition to your personal study, you can talk with priests and pastors about this. And if there is a monastery or convent near where you live, you may want to visit with leaders there—and perhaps even stay for some days of retreat. The point is simply that you do not want to rush into a decision of this magnitude. Some have done this, later realizing they were reacting to a temporary inspiration rather than to a divine call. But at the same time, it is true that in times of renewal God does call some men and women into a classical monastic expression of their discipleship.

Another possibility for living in order is to become an affiliate member of one of the historic orders. This is done by becoming an oblate in the order and attaching yourself to an existing community. If there is a monastery or convent in your area, you can easily find out how to affiliate with the community. You will go through a period of discernment and a time of novitiate prior to becoming a member, and this will give you plenty of time and exposure before you make a final decision. Most orders and communities have lay, domestic expressions.

Finally, you may simply want to start your own order. Christian history shows this occurs in times of renewal. In my own tradition, John Wesley chose to do this by establishing the United Societies, from which

Methodism emerged both as a movement and later as a family of denominations. In the following meditations I will speak more specifically about this holy but challenging process. For now, I simply want to identify it as an option. In contemporary language we would probably think of this option as small-group ministry, or what some call "accountable discipleship." The nature of this option (as we will see) is more than randomness and informality; it is life together within the context of a group covenant. Far from being a fellowship that arises and continues on the basis of subjectivism or personal preference, it is a community that forms with specific commitments and that expresses itself in agreed-upon manifestations of common life.

Living in order provides us with key ingredients in the Christian spiritual life. It provides us with substance through a directed exploration of Scripture and tradition. It provides stability by establishing a communal rule of life. It provides support as we live daily in the world through our routines and roles. It provides a sustained experience by placing us together on a journey that may well last for the rest of our lives. Living in order is a more intentional commitment to growth in grace than simply signing up for informative and inspiring studies, volunteering on short-term mission trips, or holding offices in the congregation. Living in order does not deny the value of these things, but it seeks to put them in the context of ongoing formation, not event-oriented formation.

An old phrase captures the challenge: "Christianity is so daily." Indeed! But that is because it is Life, not religion. The Christian religion is only the way we organize and express life in Christ. The Life itself is continuous. As we have noted in previous meditations, this discovery in and of itself can be transformative. When it is, the need for living in order is essential and immediate. Otherwise, we will be like the seed that fell on rocky ground—it sprang up, but because it fell among rocks, it withered. Living in order is allowing the Seed of God (via the indwelling Christ) to land in our lives in the "good soil," where it can find rootage, nourishment, and fruitfulness.

Leadership in Order

I wrestled with whether to talk next about leadership in an order or to talk more broadly about membership in one. I have decided to begin with leadership because I have found that it is where spiritual orders, small groups, and other faith communities live or die. Good leaders bless community. Bad leaders poison it. Talk to any member of a historic order and they will tell you that there is no more crucial decision than to discern who should serve the community as abbot or abbess.

Leaders in groups that experience and promote God's new pentecost are selected from among the general membership. On rare occasions historic orders have reached out beyond their own community to call someone to lead them. But the general conviction is their belief that the leader is living among them. This conviction not only directs a search process; it also defines the atmosphere in which the members live together.

An old story puts it this way. As an abbot was dying, he called the monks together to give them a final word. Last words were cherished in the monastery, but none of those who came to the abbot's bedside were expecting to hear what he was about to tell them. In words just above a whisper he said, "The Messiah is living among you." And with those words hanging in the air, he died. As the old tale goes, those six words transformed the monks' life together. They began to treat each other as if that other were the Messiah. The love and good will changed them all. And in that experience they went on to find another from their ranks to serve as the next abbot.

This is at least one reason why a commitment to leadership actually precedes a description of membership. Leaders in new pentecost orders emerge in and arise from the general membership. Some groups do not choose a leader immediately. They live together, pray together, study together, and work together for a while. They share leadership duties in the early days, waiting and watching for the person God will reveal to be their leader. They look for the person who "is Christ" to them—which means the one who clearly manifests the fruit of the Spirit. They look for a person who makes the weakest member feel secure and loved. They look for a person who confesses his own sins as well as hears the confession of others. They look for someone who is transparent and teachable. They look for a woman or man who is on the journey with the rest of the community, not just instructing others about the journey.

Most of all, they look for someone whose desire is to see everyone in the group achieve his or her unique potential in Christlikeness. Many groups have been destroyed by a leader whose agenda (usually unspoken) was to see how quickly others could become as "spiritual" as he or she claimed to be. Many groups have been suffocated by an imposed standard that the leader created to say, in effect, "Here's what I am doing. Let's see how quickly you can get up to speed and do it too." Many groups have operated on a shame system, where the only option is to do everything that's expected or to report our failure to do so. To put it simply, some groups have become sick because they were led by sick people.

We have additional guidance from ancient monasticism. The Rule of St. Benedict devotes several chapters to the life and work of the abbot. Taken together, they reveal that the leader is to be their loving shepherd, who teaches and pastors in ways that enable each member to thrive and to grow in the grace and knowledge of the Lord Jesus Christ. The Rule also reveals that the leader lives in the constant remembrance that he or she will be judged by the content or quality of his or her leadership. This means not merely drawing the circle of accountability, but living within it. It means both guiding and guarding the sheep. It means exhorting the faithful to ongoing growth, admonishing the languishing to a renewal of love and good works, restoring those who have slipped away from fidelity to their own vows, and even allowing a few to leave the community when they can no longer (or should no longer) remain in it.

As Christianity developed, this kind of leadership became referred to as "the cure of souls." Leaders take their cue from the Great Physician. Jesus helps us see sin as disease, and he guides us to see that salvation is a form of soul healing. We lead as those who can accurately diagnose the problem and adequately prescribe the medicine to cure it. Furthermore, good physicians are those who do not simply "prescribe," but who also promise to stick with their patients until the needed healing has taken place.

Much has been written about leadership in my lifetime, and I have benefited greatly from what I have read. But I have also observed that a lot of what has been written has been drawn from or based upon lessons of leadership from the business and professional world. I do not deny the reality of transferable concepts. But I do believe that leadership in a new pentecost must primarily be defined from a Christian base that is informed by Scripture and tradition. I am afraid that we turn too quickly to "the outside world" for our cues, rather than doing the longer and harder work of discovering and uncovering what our own history has to teach us.

For example, we may discover the importance of character in leadership from the professional world, but we define character by the One who incarnated it. We may learn many of the skill sets that make us effective leaders, but we learn from our faith the spirit that keeps our skills from being toxic. We may learn from the professional world how to be active, but we learn how to be authentic from our rabbi, Jesus.

It may be that some groups will want to begin their life together by a prayerful study of these biblical qualities, so that their choice of an eventual leader can be informed and inspired by the witness of the saints. But however each group may be guided, it is a holy privilege and sacred responsibility to be simultaneously intentional and careful in the selection of our leaders.

Membership in Order

The great danger in a new pentecost is enthusiasm. No movement of God has ever been sustained because people were "excited" about it. Whatever emotion there may be in our initial experience of a fresh wind of God's Spirit, the continued existence must be based on, empowered by, and directed toward other things. So, I need to say right at the beginning of this meditation: membership is not based upon those who say, "Oh, boy! I've been looking for something like this." In fact, these people may turn out to be the greatest obstacles to living in order.

I do not offer this as an indictment of anyone, for emotion will never be absent from an authentic encounter with God. But no community must allow passion to deteriorate into emotionalism. The Christian experience includes feelings, but it must also include faith—which sometimes (as we have seen in the "dark night") proceeds when all emotional sensibility has been stripped from the soul. Membership in a new pentecost community cannot be founded on feelings.

But let me hasten to say that membership is not exclusivistic. People can become members due to an initially intense emotional experience, but they must do so with a clear understanding that the community does not exist to "keep them feeling good." People who come into membership through the doorway of affection must understand that the emerging life together will include more than that. Similarly, the cognitive folks who are attracted because of the "idea" of a renewed Christian life must be clear that they will be challenged to grow in additional ways. All members must understand that the group exists to discover and develop abundant

Life. Let's consider some of the elements that give shape to this kind of membership.

Whenever possible, a new community should place itself under the supervision of an already established person or group. The first mark of a healthy group is that it seeks to be accountable. In some cases, it may be possible to do this through an institutional entity, such as a denomination or a historic spiritual order. In other cases, the new community will be under the supervision of a local pastor who is already leading an established congregation. Communities in God's new pentecost understand that there is no such thing as "independent Christianity." Members will not be those who are trying to avoid the church or trying to start their own substitute churches.

Second, the initial gathering will spend whatever time is necessary to develop a rule of life. No community can be sustained on experience alone, and still less upon emotionalism or enthusiasm. Historic monasticism has confirmed time and again that communities that either lack a rule of life or ignore an existing one will soon become subject to individuals and perspectives that will eventually undermine the maturity of the group. Christian history reveals periodic times of monastic renewal, and each time it is in relation to the recovery of order and discipline.

Third, once the rule is written and approved, all members will be viewed as novices, and they should be given an agreed-upon amount of time to live into the life of the community. Membership will never be automatic for anyone. All will "surrender for a season" to be sure that their initial attraction to the community is, in fact, a call from God. In most cases, the novitiate should be no less than a year. And some communities may want to follow the pattern of historic communities where there are several steps in the membership process before anything akin to final vows are made.

Fourth, the initial step of membership should consist of a person taking vows to live according to the established rule of life and to participate in the life of the new community. One of the great faults of institutional Christianity is the creation of a category called "inactive members." There are institutional reasons that have given rise to this category, but theologically speaking, there is no such thing. Everyone should be ready to be actively engaged. At the same time, there will always be those who are struggling to maintain their commitment. The designated group leader should quietly and confidentially work with any who are not fulfilling the vows they have made. Every provision should be made to restore any faltering person to devoted membership.

Fifth, following the designated period of the novitiate, a community should conduct a service for persons who are ready to make permanent vows. The group leader should inquire of each candidate whether he or she is ready to make this significant change in membership status. The service itself should emphasize the surrender of the persons to God, asking for grace to be disciples for the long haul. The service will be one of celebration and commitment. It will be an occasion of both dying and rising.

Sixth, the community will design and plan for annual covenant renewal. Members will be encouraged to enter into prayer and fasting prior to this renewal in order to prepare their hearts for a recommitment to Christ and to life together in the group. For others, who have concluded that they no longer should remain in the community, there will come a necessary "exit point." The renewal service is a good time to provide for a sacred "farewell."

Within these fundamental steps, a new monasticism emphasizes the need for stability. One of the historic problems faced by monastic communities is the "coming and going" of persons who essentially live their discipleship by avoiding serious accountability and long-term investment. In denominations we call them "church hoppers," but they can exist in sub-units as well. No one should be admitted into a novitiate without knowing that he or she is expected to participate in a time of testing and that ongoing membership will be based upon spiritual direction and discernment. If people violate stability and "move on" somewhere else, they should understand that returning to the community will be a difficult and prolonged process.

I can easily imagine that these elements of membership will seem harsh to many today. Some ecclesial bodies have become so inclusive that standards of membership are minimized. Many churches admit members but have absolutely nothing afterward to insure that the initial commitments remain real and growing. The new monasticism is not based upon legalism, but neither is it founded on minimalism. Life together is best begun and sustained by intentionality and accountability. To be sure, there are risks when disciplined living is undertaken. But I believe there are greater dangers when groups try to exist and sustain themselves with few or no expectations. The easiest commitment to break is one that has never really been made.

On the other hand, there is great strength and joy in being a member of a fellowship where a serious commitment to discipleship is found. And when such a community exists there is significant support and direction, which benefits each individual member in his or her desire to love God and neighbor. It is always a good thing to have an identity larger than the one we create for ourselves. Our highest identity will always be "Christian." But underneath that umbrella, we can all find enrichment and guidance by identifying ourselves with a community of people who love God and each other.

FOUR

Exalting Christ

Living in God's new pentecost is living in Christ. That's the only way to bring this book to a proper end. Peter's sermon on the Day of Pentecost was focused on Jesus. Before he ascended, Jesus said that when the Spirit comes "he will glorify me" (John 16:14). Jesus also said that when he is lifted up, he will draw all people to himself (John 12:32). When the wind of the Spirit blows, it removes the dust that settles onto our image of Christ, dulling our perceptions of him and undermining our commitments to him. Many things occur when the Spirit blows, but I will highlight only a few in this closing meditation.

First, we discover the mind of Christ. Jesus' "mind" was fundamentally his disposition toward God, others, and himself. With respect to God, we catch the spirit of surrendered service. With respect to others, we see his spirit of compassion. And with respect to himself, we see a spirit of humble confidence, which produced a resolute commitment to do the Father's will rather than his own. We exalt Christ when we have the same mind in ourselves.

Second, we experience the heart of Christ. We touched on his heart above when we used the word *compassion* in relation to him. But the heart is more than deep emotion; it is the core of a person's being. When we see the heart of Christ, we see who he was in his fundamental identity, not simply in his acts of ministry. One of the best places to see that identity is in the "I Am" statements in the Gospel of John. We exalt Christ when we live from a core identity, and not from a circumference of disconnected selves.

Third, we observe the work of Christ. I spoke of this earlier in the book, but now is a good time to return to it. The "work" of Christ (which gave rise to his works) was to find and follow the will of God. He did this through regular periods of prayerful communion with the Father. Prayer is the "work." We exalt Christ when we establish a life of prayer as the fundamental act in our lives—both individually and collectively.

Living in God's new pentecost is about exalting Christ. But we must not leave this meditative moment without pondering the word *exalt*. When Jesus refers to his exaltation in John 12:32, it is in relation to the cross. We cannot miss this. Neither can we omit this aspect from our consideration of living in a new pentecost as disciples. Jesus' exaltation was in the context of his absolute surrender to the will of God—his singular devotion to God. His exaltation was in the context of his humiliation, which included a deep sense of having been forsaken.

Historians may look back upon our age and write that our primal failure in the church was making Christianity too "quick and easy." I believe our flaw in equating prosperity with material blessing will eventually be exposed. Our tendency to settle for membership instead of discipleship will be revealed. We will be without excuse, because we who have seen the way of the cross have turned from it toward a substitute of our own making.

But in rejecting the cross, we will also have missed the source of our greatest joy. For we find it also being said of Jesus, "For the joy that was set before him, he endured the cross, despising its shame" (Heb 12:2). By rejecting the cross, we will have failed to find the real meaning of joy, which is nothing other than doing the will of God on earth as it is in heaven. By rejecting the cross, we will have separated ourselves from the great cloud of witnesses who knew, as the old hymn puts it, "the way of the cross leads home."

Living in God's new pentecost is Christ-centered. It is living *by* Christ, *with* Christ, *in* Christ, and *for* Christ. It is living in the church, his Body, and in the sub-units that accompany and shape our discipleship. It is stepping into the Stream that has been flowing for thousands of years, rather than sitting on the bank writing the story to suit our tastes and cater to our egotism. Living in God's new pentecost is a deliberate decision, which is then followed by a host of ongoing attitudes and actions that enable us to be long-haul disciples. If this book helps you gain a vision for this kind of Christianity and provides you with some guidance in establishing and maintaining it, I will have accomplished my purpose in writing it.

I'm going to ask you to consider ending your reading in prayer, using the words of a prayer that comes from the Wesleyan Covenant Service but that represents the spirit and sentiment of all Christianity. It is a prayer that provides the grace to move through the doorway of discovery into the great house of God, where the means and ways of a new pentecost are further discovered and lived out:

> *I am no longer my own, but thine.*
> *Put me to what thou wilt,*
> *Rank me with whom thou wilt.*
> *Put me to doing,*
> *Put me to suffering.*
> *Let me be employed by thee*
> *Or laid aside for thee,*
> *Exalted for thee,*
> *Or brought low for thee.*
> *Let me be full,*
> *Let me be empty.*
> *Let me have all things,*
> *Let me have nothing.*
> *I freely and heartily yield all things*
> *To thy pleasure and disposal.*
> *And now, O glorious and blessed God,*
> *Father, Son, and Holy Spirit,*
> *Thou art mine, and I am thine.*
> *So be it.*
> *And the covenant which I have made on earth,*
> *Let it be ratified in heaven.*
> *Amen.*

www.ingramcontent.com/pod-product-compliance
Lightning Source LLC
Chambersburg PA
CBHW022119090426
42743CB00008B/923